THE HEINLE
Picture Dictionary
INTERMEDIATE WORKBOOK

SECOND EDITION

NATIONAL
GEOGRAPHIC
LEARNING

HEINLE
CENGAGE Learning

Australia • Brazil • Japan • Korea • Mexico • Singapore • Spain • United Kingdom • United States

The Heinle Picture Dictionary, Intermediate Workbook, Second Edition

Publisher: Sherrise Roehr

Senior Development Editor:
Jill Korey O'Sullivan

Development Editor: Brenden Layte

Director of Global Marketing:
Ian Martin

Product Marketing Manager:
Lindsey Miller

Director of Content and Media Production:
Michael Burggren

Content Project Manager: Mark Rzeszutek

Senior Print Buyer: Mary Beth Hennebury

Compositor: PreMediaGlobal

Cover Design: Michael Rosenquest

Cover Photo: Brian Skerry

Senior Technology Product Manager:
Scott Rule

Workbook + Audio CD
ISBN-13: 978-1-133-56318-1

Workbook
ISBN-13: 978-1-133-56314-3

National Geographic Learning
20 Channel Center Street
Boston, MA 02210
USA

Cengage Learning is a leading provider of customized learning solutions with office locations around the globe, including Singapore, the United Kingdom, Australia, Mexico, Brazil, and Japan.

Cengage Learning products are represented in Canada by Nelson Education, Ltd.

Visit National Geographic Learning online at: **ngl.cengage.com**
Visit our corporate website at **cengage.com**

Printed in the United States of America
1 2 3 4 5 6 7 8 9 15 14

Credits

Illustrators

Cheryl Kirk Noll/CATugeau LLC: pp. 115, 117
Bob Kayganich/IllustrationOnLine.com: pp. 11–12, 71, 79, 143, 154
Greg LaFever/Scott Hull Associates Inc.: pp. 83 (top), 189
Precision Graphics: pp. 3 (A–D), 55, 169, 175, 193
Susan Spellman/Gwen Walters Artist Representative: pp. 75
Carol Stutz Illustration: pp. 113, 145, 163
Gary Torrisi/Gwen Walters Artist Representative: pp. 81, 120, 130 (bottom), 131
Meryl Treatner/CATugeau LLC: pp. 108–110, 111 (bottom), 133 (1–3)

Photos

Unit One – Unit One Opener: ©Tom Grill/Corbis; 2: ©Hemera Photo-Objects; 7: ©Photos.com/RF; 9: ©Hemera Photo-Objects; 10: ©Hemera Photo-Objects, ©Jupiterimages/Photos.com; 14: ©IndexOpen; 17: ©IndexOpen, ©Mihai Simonia/Shutterstock.com, ©Corbis

Unit Two – Unit Two Opener: ©Royalty-Free/Corbis; 19: ©Photos.com; 21: ©IndexOpen, ©Photos.com; 23: ©IndexOpen; 24: ©Hemera Photo-Objects, © cristi180884/Shutterstock.com

Unit Three – Unit Three Opener: ©Thinkstock/Getty Images; 26: ©Photos.com, ©IndexOpen, 27: ©IndexOpen; 29: ©IndexOpen; 31: ©Sunset Boulevard/Corbis

Unit Four – Unit Four Opener: © Jose Luis Pelaez, Inc./Corbis; 32: ©Photos.com; 33: ©IndexOpen; 34: ©Hemera Photo-Objects; 39: ©Photos.com; 41: ©IndexOpen, ©Photos.com; 42: ©IndexOpen

Unit Five – Unit Five Opener: ©Photodisc Collection/Getty Images; 4: ©IndexOpen, ©Photos.com, © 06photo/Shutterstock.com, ©Photos.com; 53: ©IndexOpen; 60: ©IndexOpen

Unit Six – Unit Six Opener: ©Cydney Conger/Flirt/CORBIS; 62: ©IndexOpen, ©V&A Images/Alamy, ©Photos.com; ©Hemera Photo Objects; 65: ©IndexOpen; 73: ©IndexOpen; 74: beerlogoff/Shutterstock.com 76: ©Hemera Photo-Objects, ©Photos.com; 80: ©Hemera Photo-Objects

Unit Seven – Unit Seven Opener: ©Burke-Triolo Productions/Getty Images; 83: ©IndexOpen; 84: ©Hemera Photo-Objects, ©Svetlana Foote/Shutterstock.com; 85: ©Hemera Photo-Objects, ©Photos.com; 86: ©Dani Vincek /Shutterstock.com, ©D7INAMI7S /Shutterstock.com, © HLPhoto/Shutterstock.com, ©NITI JUNKAVEEKOOL /Shutterstock.com, ©Olga Popova/Shutterstock.com, © enzo4 /Shutterstock.com, ©Patrick Robinson/Photos.com; 89: ©IndexOpen; 90: ©Hemera Photo-Objects; 91: ©Dream79 /Shutterstock.com, ©Joao Virissimo/Shutterstock.com, ©travellight /Shutterstock.com; 93: ©Hemera Photo-Objects; 95: ©Hemera Photo-Objects; 96: ©Hemera Photo-Objects; 97: ©Hemera Photo-Objects; 101: ©Hemera Photo-Objects; 103: ©Hemera Photo-Objects, ©Photos.com

Unit Eight – Unit Eight Opener: ©C Squared Studios/Getty Images; 107: ©Hemera Photo- Objects

Unit Nine – Unit Nine Opener: © Wes Thompson/Corbis; 119: ©Hemera Photo-Objects; ©Jupiterimages/Photos.com, ©Photos.com, ©Hemera Technologies/Photos.com; 126: ©Photos.com, ©IndexOpen; 129: ©IndexOpen, © Ortodox/Shutterstock.com, ©rorem/Shutterstock.com; 130: ©IndexOpen

Unit Ten – Unit Ten Opener: ©Herrmann/Starke/Corbis; 132: ©IndexOpen; 133: ©Hemera Photo-Objects, ©IndexOpen; 136: ©Hemera Photo-Objects; 139: ©IndexOpen, ©Hemera Technologies /Photos.com; 140: ©Index Open, ©Hemera Technologies /Photos.com, ©Hemera Photo-Objects; 142: ©Hemera Photo-Objects

Unit Eleven – Unit Eleven Opener: © PictureNet/Corbis; 150: ©Hemera Photo-Objects, ©IndexOpen; 152: ©Hemera Photo Objects; 157: ©Hemera Photo Objects; 158: ©Hemera Photo Objects; 160: ©Hemera Photo Objects, ©IndexOpen; 161: ©Hemera Photo Objects; 164: ©Hemera Photo Objects, ©IndexOpen

Unit Twelve – Unit Twelve Opener: © L. Clarke/Corbis; 167: ©IndexOpen; 168: ©IndexOpen, ©Photos.com, ©Hemera Technologies /Photos.com, © Ablestock.com/Photos.com; 170: ©Photos.com, ©Hemera Technologies /Photos.com, ©Ablestock.com/Photos.com, ©IndexOpen; 171: ©Hemera Technologies /Photos.com, ©IndexOpen; 173: ©Photos.com, ©IndexOpen

Unit Thirteen – Unit Thirteen Opener: ©Digital Vision/Getty Images; 179: ©Hemera Photo Objects; 181: ©Hemera Photo Objects, ©IndexOpen; 183: ©Hemera Photo-Objects, ©lendy16/Shutterstock.com; 187: ©Photos.com, ©IndexOpen, ©Hemera Technologies/Photos.com; 188: ©IndexOpen, ©Photos.com, ©Jupiterimages/Photos.com; 191: ©Hemera Photo Objects

Unit Fourteen – Unit Fourteen Opener: ©Don Farrall/Getty Images; 194: ©Photos.com, ©IndexOpen, ©IndexOpen/RF; 195: ©Hemera Photo Objects, ©Ivancovlad/Shutterstock.com, ©Jarun Ontakrai/Photos.com, ©Ablestock.com/Photos.com; 199: ©Photos.com, ©IndexOpen, ©Andrew K/epa/epa/Corbis

Unit Fifteen – Unit Fifteen Opener: ©Don Farrall/Getty Images; 203: ©Photos.com; 205: ©IndexOpen; 206: ©IndexOpen, ©Photos.com; 207: ©GWImages /Shutterstock.com, ©IndexOpen; 208: ©Photos.com, ©IndexOpen/RF

Unit Sixteen – Unit Sixteen Opener: ©Digital Vision/Getty Images; 211: ©IndexOpen, ©Photos.com; 212: ©Hemera Photo Objects, ©IndexOpen/RF; 213: ©Index Open; 215: ©IndexOpen; 217:© Hemera Photo Objects; 219: ©Hemera Photo Objects; 221: ©IndexOpen/RF; 222: ©Hemera Photo Objects; 223: ©IndexOpen; 224: ©Hemera Photo-Objects, ©IndexOpen; 225: ©Photos.com/RF, ©IndexOpen/RF, ©Hemera Photo-Objects; 228: ©IndexOpen/RF

To the Teacher

The Heinle Picture Dictionary Intermediate Workbook, Second Edition provides intermediate students with a variety of activities to practice and reinforce the vocabulary learned in *The Heinle Picture Dictionary*. The workbook can be used in conjunction with class instruction or can be used on its own. This edition of the workbook features new activities, audio, and art to go with the updated word lists presented in *The Heinle Picture Dictionary, Second edition*.

The workbook follows the same page-by-page format as *The Heinle Picture Dictionary*. For example, after introducing a spread such as City Square (pages 58–59) in the dictionary, students can complete the corresponding pages in the workbook (pages 58–59). The exercises can be done in class, in small groups, or assigned as homework.

The workbook offers a wide variety of vocabulary practice activities. Some are at the word level, for example, asking students to choose words that can follow a particular verb, selecting the two words with similar meanings, or placing words in categories. Most activities are at the sentence level. Students may write the correct vocabulary word in sentences, place steps in order, decide if statements are true or false, or decide if sentences are the same or different in meaning. In many activities, students write the correct response to questions or comments about the topic. Students are often asked to write sentences in their notebooks based on colorful, attractive photographs or illustrations related to the vocabulary topic. Each unit ends with a *Word Work* activity. Though these exercises may be done individually, they are best accomplished in a small group or with a partner. Using the vocabulary in the unit, students discuss and compare their experiences, preferences, area highlights, similarities and differences, favorite recipes, schedules, etc.

A unique and important feature of this workbook is the listening activity that appears in each lesson. The listening activities reinforce the vocabulary in a number of ways. Many listening exercises ask the students to match pictures with sentences or short dialogues.

Students might hear sentences about a picture and decide if they are true or false. In other listening activities, students answer questions about conversations, circle the correct response, identify the correct person, write prices, or follow directions. There is ample support for the listening exercises, with pictures and word boxes providing spelling assistance. It will be necessary to pause between each item in the listening exercises to allow students sufficient time to choose the correct answer. Students often find it helpful to listen to the exercises more than once. When the listening activity is done in class, students should be encouraged to listen to the CD again at home for review.

The final page of each workbook unit provides a *Word Study* box. These are vocabulary learning strategies. Learners need several exposures to a new word or phrase in order to learn it. Short practice periods with frequent review are usually more effective than long study sessions. Teachers can introduce the strategies at any time and in any order. Allow class time in which to discuss the ideas and get student feedback. Some students may have additional helpful strategies to offer the class. Students should identify two or three strategies that are effective for them. Time spent in class reflecting on how to study can help students acquire more effective learning strategies. Along with these features, the new edition of the workbook includes a *Grammar Connection* where the content of each lesson is used to teach or review an appropriate grammar point. A grammar point is presented, along with notes on its usage, before students get a chance to practice it using words from *The Heinle Picture Dictionary*.

Many students find that a personal vocabulary notebook helps them record new words and allows for quick review sessions. A sample page from such a notebook and additional suggestions for choosing and recording new words are presented on the next page.

Enjoy using *The Heinle Picture Dictionary Intermediate Workbook* in your class and watching your students' vocabulary grow!

A Vocabulary Notebook

Many students find that a vocabulary notebook is a helpful way to learn and review new vocabulary words. The sample below shows part of a potential vocabulary notebook page.

```
bald - no hair
glasses
moustache

get on (the bus)
cross (the street)
fall - caer
leave - dejar
angry
thirsty - I am thirsty. I'd like a soda.

love -

worried - preocupado

brush your teeth
comb your hair
put on makeup - maquillarse
take a nap - short sleep in the daytime
do housework - hacer las tareas de la casa
```

What words should I put in my vocabulary notebook?

This is *your* personal notebook. Put in words *you* want to remember. Write some new words from your dictionary. Add words that you see or hear in school or at work. Write words that you hear on TV or in a song you like.

How should I write the words?

Students write new words in different ways. Sometimes, you will remember the word when you see it. For other words, you can translate the word into your own language or draw a simple picture. You may also want to write a short sentence with the word or write a definition.

How can I learn new words?

There are three rules for learning new vocabulary:

Rule #1: Review.
Rule #2: Review.
Rule #3: Review again.

Contents

6 Housing

7 Food

8 Clothing

9 Transportation

15 The Arts

16 Recreation

Numbers

A **Write the number.**

a. 9 _____nine_____

b. 14 _____

c. 19 _____

d. 25 _____

e. 38 _____

f. 43 _____

g. 57 _____

h. 60 _____

i. 72 _____

j. 81 _____

k. 96 _____

l. 100 _____

Grammar Connection: Future Tense – *be going to*

I	am		
He She	is	going to be	twenty.
We You They	are		

Note:
- Use the future tense to talk about actions that are going to happen tomorrow, next week, or sometime in the future.

B **Write the age of each person on his/her/their next birthday.**

1. She is twelve. _She is going to be thirteen._

2. I am seventeen. _____

3. He is twenty. _____

4. They are twenty-nine. _____

5. She is thirty-three. _____

6. I am thirty-nine. _____

7. You are fifty-seven. _____

8. She is sixty-four. _____

9. We are seventy. _____

10. He is seventy-nine. _____

C **Match the statement with the correct graph.**

1. Three quarters of the students are studying English. _c_

2. Half of the students are studying English. _____

3. One quarter of the students are studying English. _____

4. Two thirds of the students are studying English. _____

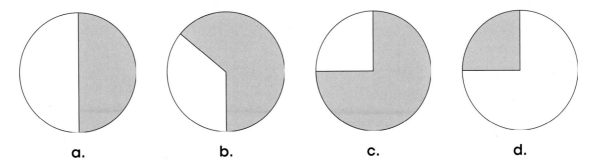

a.   b.   c.   d.

CD 1
Track 1

D **Listen and complete the forms.**

Name: _____ Jiang Xu _____

Student ID: _____

Cell Phone: _____

Name: _____ Julia Hernandez _____

Student ID: _____

Telephone Number: _____

Word Work **Small Group**

Write or discuss. Use numbers in your answers.

1. What is the address of your school?
2. How many floors are in your school building?
3. What floor is your classroom on?
4. What is your classroom number?
5. How many students are in your class? How many men? How many women?
6. About how many students are in your school?

Time

A **Match.**

  _c_   **1.** a minute   **a.** 100 years

____ **2.** an hour   **b.** 365 days

____ **3.** a day   **c.** 60 seconds

____ **4.** a week   **d.** 24 hours

____ **5.** a month   **e.** 7 days

____ **6.** a year   **f.** 60 minutes

____ **7.** a decade   **g.** 1,000 years

____ **8.** a century   **h.** 28–31 days

____ **9.** a millennium   **i.** 10 years

Grammar Connection: **Prepositions of Time – at / in**

at	in	
at 5:00	**in** the morning	today
at seven o'clock	**in** the afternoon	every day
at noon	**in** the evening	every week
at night		once a day
at midnight		twice a month

B **Complete the sentence with *at* or *in*. Write *X* if no preposition is needed.**

1. I get up _at_ six o'clock.

2. I take the bus to school ____ the morning.

3. I go to the supermarket ____ every week.

4. I eat lunch ____ noon.

5. School ends ____ 3:00.

6. I do my homework ____ the evening.

7. I exercise ____ twice a week.

8. I watch my favorite TV show ____ 9:00.

9. I use my computer ____ night.

10. I go to bed ____ midnight.

C Complete this information about yourself. Write the number of minutes, days, hours, weeks, months, or years for each sentence.

1. It takes me _____ to get to school.

2. I study vocabulary for _____ every day.

3. I sleep _____ a night.

4. I watch TV _____ a day.

5. I have _____ vacation from work/school.

6. I have been absent from school _____ this year.

7. I talk on the phone _____ a day.

8. I go to school _____ a week.

9. I have been studying English for _____.

D Listen and fill in the correct times.

CD 1
Track 2

1.
| Bank |
| 9 : 00 to ____ : ____ |

2.
| Library |
| ____ : ____ to ____ : ____ |

3.
| Restaurant |
| ____ : ____ to ____ : ____ |

4.
| Supermarket |
| ____ : ____ to ____ : ____ |

5.
| Post Office |
| ____ : ____ to ____ : ____ |

6.
| Barbershop |
| ____ : ____ to ____ : ____ |

Word Work Small Group

Answer each question. Then, discuss your answers with your group. Complete the sentences with the name of a student in your group.

1. What time do you get up? _____ _____ gets up the earliest.

2. What time do you go to bed? _____ _____ goes to bed the latest.

3. What hours do you work? _____ _____ works the most hours.

4. What hours do you sleep? _____ _____ sleeps the longest.

Calendar

A   **Write the day for each abbreviation.**

1. Tues. _____Tuesday_____   4. Wed. _____

2. Fri. _____   5. Sat. _____

3. Sun. _____   6. Thurs. _____

B   **Write the next month.**

1. February _____March_____   5. December _____

2. May _____   6. April _____

3. October _____   7. January _____

4. August _____   8. June _____

Grammar Connection: Prepositions of Time – *in / on*

in	on	
in September	**on** Sunday	today
in the summer	**on** Tuesday	tomorrow
in the winter	**on** September 10	yesterday
in 1998	**on** July 4	

C   **Complete the sentence with *in* or *on*. Write *X* if no preposition is needed.**

1. I got my driver's license __in__ May.

2. We don't have school __X__ tomorrow.

3. I have a doctor's appointment ____ Wednesday.

4. We don't have classes ____ the summer.

5. I got married ____ June 21st.

6. We went to the park ____ yesterday.

7. My birthday is ____ November.

8. I don't work ____ Sunday.

9. It's very cold ____ the winter.

10. My vacation begins ____ August 1st.

D Complete the sentence with the name of a month.

1. My birthday is in _____.

2. People celebrate Christmas in _____.

3. School begins in _____ and ends in _____.

4. _____ is the coldest month of the year.

5. _____ is the hottest month of the year.

6. _____ is my favorite month.

E Write the date. Use this form: month/day/year.

1. February 22, 2014 _2/22/2014_   5. July 1, 2006 _____

2. May 4, 1997 _____   6. December 10, 2021 _____

3. October 15, 1950 _____   7. August 18, 1948 _____

4. March 14, 2015 _____   8. January 7, 2010 _____

CD 1
Track 3

F Listen and write the month of each holiday from around the world.

1. Japan celebrates Tanabata on _____ 7th.

2. In India, people celebrate Diwali in _____.

3. New Year's is usually in _____ in China.

4. Cinco de Mayo on _____ 5th
   is a popular holiday in Mexico.

5. _____ 13th is Santa Lucia,
   a national holiday in Sweden.

6. South Africa celebrates National Woman's Day
   on _____ 9th.

7. _____ 23rd is Children's Day in Turkey.

Word Work Small Group

Write three dates that are important in your life, such as your birthday, anniversary, a graduation, etc. Read the dates to your classmates. Explain why each date is important to you.

1. _____   2. _____   3. _____

Money and Shopping

A **Write the coins and bills each person will receive as change.**

1. Joseph buys a stamp for forty cents. He gives the clerk a dollar.

   Change: ___*a dime and two quarters*___

2. Ana buys a cup of coffee for $1.20. She gives the clerk $1.50.

   Change: _____

3. Hoang buys a notebook for $3.79. He gives the clerk five dollars.

   Change: _____

4. Raj buys headphones for $12.60. He gives the clerk twenty dollars.

   Change: _____

Grammar Connection: Simple Present Tense

I You We They	**shop** **don't shop**	online.
He She	**shops** **doesn't shop**	online.

Note:
- The simple present tense tells about everyday actions.
- In affirmative statements, add *s* on the verb after *he, she,* and *it.*

B **Complete the sentences with the correct form of the simple present tense.**

1. He always (use) ___*uses*___ cash. He (negative/use) ___*doesn't use*___ a credit card.

2. In this state, people (pay) _____ sales tax on clothes. They (negative/pay)

   _____ sales tax on food.

3. She (use) _____ coupons, so she (save) _____ money at the supermarket.

4. I sometimes (return) _____ items, so I (keep) _____ my receipts.

5. She (have) _____ a debit card. She (negative/have) _____ a credit card.

6. I (shop) _____ during sales. I (negative/pay) _____ full price for things.

c **Write the price of each item.**

$ 1.*00*   _____   _____   _____

_____   _____   _____   _____

D **Complete the conversation between the cashier and the shopper on page 9 of the dictionary. Write the correct answer after each question.**

The regular price is $36.00.	The sale price is $27.00.
~~Yes, they are.~~	No, we only accept cash and credit cards.
Yes, but you need your receipt.	

1. Are these hats on sale today?
   Yes, they are.
   _____

2. How much is this hat?
   _____

3. How much is the sale price?
   _____

4. Can I pay by check?
   _____

5. Can I return the hat?
   _____

Word Work **Small Group**

Are you a smart shopper? Circle *Yes* or *No* for each statement. Then, discuss each item with your group. Which students in your group are smart shoppers?

1. I try to buy things on sale.   Yes   No
2. I always check my receipt.   Yes   No
3. I always keep my receipt.   Yes   No
4. I have one or two credit cards.   Yes   No
5. I always pay with cash.   Yes   No
6. I check the prices in two or three stores. Yes   No

Colors

A Write the names of the colors you see in each picture.

1. The colors in the picture of the hot air balloon are <u>red,</u>

   _____ .

2. The colors in the picture of the parrot are _____ .

   _____

Grammar Connection: **Adverbs of Frequency**

always	95 – 100%
usually	80 – 99%
often	60 – 80%
sometimes	20 – 80%
rarely	2 – 5%
never	0 – 2%

Note:
- Put adverbs of frequency after *be*
- Put the adverb of frequency before the verb.

B Complete the sentences with an adverb of frequency.

1. A school bus is <u>usually</u> yellow.

2. A police car is _____ black and white.

3. A fire engine is _____ pink.

4. A fire hydrant is _____ red or yellow.

5. A stop sign is _____ red.

6. A traffic light is _____ blue.

7. An ambulance is _____ white.

8. A taxi is _____ turquoise.

C Complete the sentences with color words.

1. _____ is a common color for cars.

2. _____ is a dull color for a classroom.

3. _____ is a lively color for a classroom.

4. _____ is a strange color for a house.

5. _____ is a relaxing color for a bedroom.

6. My bedroom is _____.

7. I look good in _____.

8. I don't look good in _____.

9. My favorite color is _____.

CD 1
Track 5

D Listen to the description of each boy's clothing. Write each name next to the correct boy.

| Ben | Jesse | Jason | Todd | Sam | Kyle |

Ben

Word Work Small Group

Complete the sentences. Then, read your sentences to one another.
What information is the same? What information is different?

1. At a wedding, the bride usually wears a _____ dress.

2. At a funeral, people often wear _____.

3. The _____ are my favorite sports team. They wear _____ uniforms.

4. I look good in _____.

5. _____ is my favorite color.

In, On, Under

A Complete these sentences with the correct prepositions.

1. There are nine cars _____ *on* _____ the truck.

2. The white car is _____ the red car and the silver car.

3. The red car is _____ the white car.

4. The silver car is _____ the white car.

5. The green car is _____ the silver car.

6. The blue car is _____ the black car.

7. The black car is _____ the sports car.

8. The sports car has a ribbon _____ it.

9. One man is driving the brown car _____ the truck.

10. The woman is standing _____ the truck.

11. The two men are _____ the truck.

12. The cat is _____ the truck.

B Match the opposites.

_c_	**1.** in front of	**a.** underneath
___	**2.** outside of	**b.** far from
___	**3.** on top of	**c.** behind
___	**4.** on the left of	**d.** inside of
___	**5.** near	**e.** on the right of

Grammar Connection: *Who* and *What* as Subjects

Who is sitting in front of you?	**Aisha is.**
Who is standing?	**The teacher is.**
What is on your desk?	**My books are.**

C **Answer the questions.**

1. Who is in front of you? _____
2. What is under your desk? _____
3. What is in your hand? _____
4. Who is near you? _____
5. Who is behind you? _____
6. What is on the floor? _____

CD 1
Track 6

D **Listen to each statement about the desk. Circle *True* or *False*.**

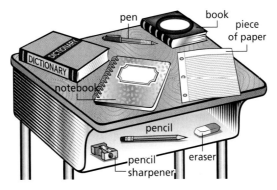

1. True (False)	**4.** True False	**7.** True False
2. True False	**5.** True False	**8.** True False
3. True False	**6.** True False	**9.** True False

Word Work **Small Group**

Read the description of a bookcase. On a piece of paper, draw the bookcase and the items. Then, sit in a group and compare your pictures.

I have a small bookcase in my room. On the top of the bookcase is a small TV. The remote control is on the right. On the top shelf, there are two photographs of my family on the left. On the right is a box with a lot more photographs inside. On the middle shelf there are two small speakers, one on the left and one on the right. My camera and lenses are between the speakers. On the bottom shelf there are a lot of books. Next to the books is a box of tissues. There is a wastebasket beside the bookshelf on the right.

Opposites

A Write two sentences about each picture. Use the new words in your dictionary.

 **1.**    **2.**    **3.**

1. _____

2. _____

3. _____

Grammar Connection: *Too*

It's **too noisy**. I can't study
It's **too hot** outside. Let's go inside.

Note:
- Use *too* before an adjective.
- You can use *too* to express a negative idea or problem.

B Complete the sentences with *too* and an adjective.

young	hard	hot	full
short	expensive	~~difficult~~	slow

1. I don't understand this math problem. It's _____*too difficult*_____.

2. I can't reach the top shelf. I'm _____.

3. Don't eat the soup yet. It's _____.

4. He won't win the race. He's _____.

5. I can't buy that camera. It's _____.

6. She's only fourteen. She's _____.

7. I can't eat any more pizza. I'm _____.

8. This pillow isn't comfortable. It's _____.

c **Answer the question in a complete sentence.**

1. Are you going to buy a small camera or a large camera?

   _____

2. Is she going to marry a rich man or a poor man?

   _____

3. Do you like a hard pillow or a soft pillow?

   _____

4. Do you like hot days or cold days?

   _____

5. Do you live in a quiet area or a noisy area?

   _____

6. Is your car usually clean or dirty?

   _____

CD 1
Track 7

D **Listen and circle the letter of the correct sentence.**

1. **a.** She's young.   **b.** She's old.

2. **a.** It's full.   **b.** It's empty.

3. **a.** She's weak.   **b.** She's strong.

4. **a.** It's cold.   **b.** It's hot.

5. **a.** It's noisy.   **b.** It's quiet.

6. **a.** It's new.   **b.** It's old.

7. **a.** They're clean.   **b.** They're dirty.

8. **a.** He's poor.   **b.** He's rich.

Word Work **Small Group**

Complete the sentences with adjectives. Talk about your answers with your group.
1. I prefer _____ weather.
2. I prefer to live in a _____, _____ area.
3. I prefer a _____ chair.
4. I prefer to marry a _____, _____ man/woman.

The Telephone

A   **Match the questions and the answers.**

    _b_ **1.** What's the number for emergency assistance?   **a.** $5, $10, or $20

    ____ **2.** What's the number for information?   **b.** 911

    ____ **3.** How many time zones are there in the United States?   **c.** 305

    ____ **4.** What's your telephone number?   **d.** 411

    ____ **5.** What's the area code for Miami?   **e.** 555-4545

    ____ **6.** How much is a calling card?   **f.** four

Grammar Connection: Future Tense with *going to*

I	am		
You We They	are	going to	call 911.
He She	is		

Note:
- The future tense tells about things you plan to do tomorrow, next week, or some time in the future.

B   **Read the situation. What is each person going to do? Use the future tense.**

1. Jason doesn't know the phone number. (look it up)

    He is going to look it up.

2. Christina is in her car. She wants to make a phone call. (use her headset)

    _____

3. Mr. and Mrs. Patel just saw an accident. (call 911)

    _____

4. Paula wants to change her cell phone plan. (call the phone company)

    _____

5. Your phone is ringing. (answer it)

    _____

C What is each person doing? Write a sentence about each picture in your notebook.

a.

b.

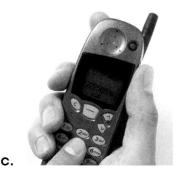
c.

CD 1
Track 8

D Listen to each sound or speaker. What is happening? Write the number of each sound or speaker next to the correct sentence.

_____ **a.** The phone is ringing.

_____ **b.** She's answering the phone.

__1__ **c.** She's dialing a number.

_____ **d.** He's making an international call.

_____ **e.** He's asking for directory assistance.

Word Work **Small Group**

Complete the information. Then, talk about your cell phones.
1. I have / don't have a cell phone.
2. I talk on the phone about _____ minutes a day.
3. I text about _____ times a day.
4. Cell phone provider (company) I use: _____
5. Cell phone plan: _____ text messages, _____ voice minutes
6. How many people in your family are on the plan? _____
7. What greeting do you have on your voicemail? _____

Word Study

There are many ways to study new vocabulary words. Some students learn by writing, some students say the words out loud, some students like to use an audio CD and repeat words, and other students study with a partner. How do you learn new words? Listen to other students give suggestions. Try several different methods.

Classroom

A **Complete the sentences.**

1. For your _____, please complete pages 18 and 19.

2. A _____ is round. It shows the countries of the world.

3. You write on a whiteboard with a _____.

4. You write on a blackboard with _____.

5. His _____ on the test was 90%.

6. Study hard. We have a big _____ tomorrow.

7. Please put the book on the _____.

Grammar Connection: *There is / There are*

There is	**a** student in the classroom.
There are	**nine** students in the classroom.

Note:
- A sentence beginning with *There is* or *There are* often tells how many.
- Use *There is* with a singular subject.
- Use *There are* with a plural subject.

B **Complete the sentences with *There is* or *There are*.**

1. _____There are_____ many books on the bookshelf.

2. _____ a teacher at the whiteboard.

3. _____ five desks in this classroom.

4. _____ six flags on the bulletin board.

5. _____ a clock over the bulletin board.

6. _____ a globe on the bookcase.

7. _____ many chairs in the classroom.

C **Complete the sentences.**

high school	college	~~international~~	graduate

1. An _____international_____ student is a student from another country.

2. A _____ student is often between the ages of 18 and

22 years old. He chooses a major such as business, art, or science.

3. A _____ student is usually between 14 and 18 years old. She usually lives at home with her parents.

4. A _____ student continues to study after college.

D **Write the sentence with a similar meaning.**

> She failed the test.
> She studied for the test.
> She cheated on the test.
> She took a test.
> ~~She passed the test.~~

1. She got 100% on her test.   _____She passed the test._____

2. She got 55% on her test.   _____

3. She copied from another student.   _____

4. She looked at her notes carefully.   _____

5. She had an exam.   _____

E **Listen and write the number of each question before the correct answer.**

CD 1
Track 9

____ **a.** Let's look at a map.

____ **b.** Her name is Ms. Jackson.

____ **c.** I got an A.

____ **d.** It's on the bookcase.

____ **e.** I don't know. There's a clock in the classroom.

____ **f.** Do pages 18 and 19 in your workbook.

__1__ **g.** It's on the blackboard.

Word Work   **Small Group**

Write the names of ten items in your classroom.
Write a sentence describing the location of each item.
Examples: **The clock is over the door.**
The blackboard is in front of the classroom.

Listen, Read, Write

> **Go** to the board.
> **Write** your name.

Note:
• When you give instructions, use the base form of the verb.

A **Circle the two words that can follow each verb.**

1. hand out: (the books)   (the papers)   the sentence
2. copy: the word   the group   the sentence
3. write: the dictionary   your name   your answer
4. spell: the board   the word   your name
5. talk with: your book   your group   your partner
6. erase: the board   the word   the pencil

B **Write a sentence that has the same meaning.**

> discuss   raise   ~~hand out~~
> hand in   copy   look up

1. Give the papers to the students. _____ **Hand out the papers.** _____
2. Find the word in the dictionary. _____
3. Write this sentence. _____
4. Put up your hand. _____
5. Talk about your ideas. _____
6. Give me your papers. _____

C **Follow the directions.**

1. Underline the correct answer.
   10 + 20 =   10   20   <u>30</u>

2. Cross out the wrong answers.
   5 + 5 + 7 =   10   17   27

3. Fill in the blank.
   15 – 5 = _____

4. Circle the correct answer.
   4 + 15 =   11   18   19

5. Darken the correct oval.
   11 + 12 =   ○ 23   ○ 24   ○ 25

6. Check the correct answer.
   12 + 9 =   ___ 20   ___ 21   ___ 22

CD 1
Track 10

D Listen and write the directions you hear.

1. _Open your books to page 21._

2. _____

3. _____

4. _____

5. _____

6. _____

7. _____

E Look at the classroom pictures. On another piece of paper, write about each picture. Describe what the students are doing.

Word Work **Partners**

How do you like to study a new language? Check the activities that you find helpful. Then, add your own idea. Compare your answers with your partner's.

☐ **1.** I like to write sentences.

☐ **2.** I like to copy new words.

☐ **3.** I like to listen to the new language.

☐ **4.** I like to talk with a group.

☐ **5.** I like to read in the new language.

☐ **6.** I like to look up new words in the dictionary.

☐ **7.** I like to do exercises, such as fill-in and matching.

8. I like to _____.

School

A **Write the correct person.**

1. This person manages a school. _____a principal_____

2. This person calls a parent when a child is sick. _____

3. This person helps students plan their schedules. _____

4. This person manages a sports team. _____

5. These students play a sport together. _____

B **Complete the places and items you find in a school.**

1. permission _____slip_____   5. guidance _____

2. language _____   6. report _____

3. water _____   7. teachers' _____

4. absence _____   8. drama _____

Grammar Connection: **Present Progressive Tense**

I	am	
He It	is	waving. dancing. smiling.
We You They	are	

Note:
- The present progressive tense tells about an action that is happening now.

C **Complete the sentences in the present progressive tense. Then, write the correct location.**

1. They ____are eating____ (eat) lunch in the ____cafeteria____.

2. They _____ (practice) for graduation in the _____.

3. She _____ (write) a report in the _____.

4. They _____ (play) basketball in the _____.

5. We _____ (take) an English class in the _____.

6. She _____ (listen) to Spanish conversations in the _____.

7. He _____ (get) a cup of coffee in the _____.

D Complete the sentences.

1. The principal makes the announcements on the ___loudspeaker___.

2. A _____ shows a student's classes, with the days and times.

3. When a child is sick, a parent writes an _____.

4. Students carry their books to school in _____.

5. Students sit on _____ to watch sports in the gym.

6. A parent signs a _____ to allow a child to go on a class trip.

7. Students keep their coats and books in their _____.

8. A _____ gives a student's grades in each subject.

9. Students who live far from school take the _____.

10. Students listen to speakers and watch movies in the _____.

E Listen to each statement. Where is each student?

CD 1
Track 11

1. ___cafeteria___
2. _____
3. _____
4. _____
5. _____
6. _____
7. _____
8. _____
9. _____

Word Work Partners

Write your school schedule. How is your schedule the same as your partner's? How is it different?

Computers

A Write the name of each computer component.

1. *a laptop* 2. _____ 3. _____ 4. _____

5. _____ 6. _____ 7. _____ 8. _____

Grammar Connection: *I know how to / I don't know how to*

I know how to I don't know how to	connect to the Internet. open an e-mail.

Note:
- To talk about your skills, use *I know how to* and *I don't know how to*.
- Use the base form of the verb after *know how to*.

B Write about your skills with the computer. Use *I know how to* or *I don't know how to*.

1. I ___*don't know how to*___ scan a document.

2. I _____ print a document.

3. I _____ send an e-mail.

4. I _____ save my work on a flash drive.

5. I _____ change my password.

6. I _____ connect my computer to a projector.

7. I _____ find all my files.

C Cross out the word that does not belong.

1. **a.** CD-ROM   **b.** ~~toolbar~~   **c.** flash drive

2. **a.** cable   **b.** file   **c.** folder

3. **a.** laptop   **b.** tablet   **c.** an e-mail

4. **a.** mouse   **b.** scanner   **c.** mouse pad

5. **a.** projector   **b.** keyboard   **c.** key

6. **a.** monitor   **b.** screen   **c.** printer

D Write the correct word.

a tablet	a cursor	a mouse
a keyboard	an e-mail	the Internet
a flash drive	a cable	a printer

1. You can save a lot of information on it.   _**a flash drive**_

2. You type on it. _____

3. You can print a report on it. _____

4. A friend sends you it. _____

5. It moves the cursor. _____

6. This portable computer uses a touch screen. _____

7. It connects computers around the world. _____

8. This arrow points to your location on the screen. _____

9. It connects a printer to a computer. _____

E Listen and complete the directions.

CD 1
Track 12

1. Press a _____.

2. Send an _____.

3. _____ on an icon.

4. _____ the text.

5. Open a _____.

6. _____ a picture.

7. Insert a _____.

8. _____ your password.

9. Surf the _____.

10. Attach the _____.

Word Study

Study vocabulary for short periods of time, for example, ten minutes twice a day. The more frequently you see and practice a word, the more likely you are to remember it.

Family

a.   b.   o.

A **A family member is describing his/her family. Choose the picture that shows his/her family.**

1. I'm a single father. _____a_____

2. I have four sisters. _____

3. I live with my grandmother and grandfather. _____

4. We have two daughters. _____

5. My mother-in-law is helpful with the children. _____

6. My parents live with my wife and me. _____

7. We have two children. _____ and _____

8. I have an older brother. _____ and _____

Grammar Connection: Possessive Nouns

My uncle is my **mother's** brother.
My cousin is my **uncle's** child.

Note:
* Use 's after a name to show possession.

B **Complete the sentences with a possessive noun.**

1. My grandmother is my _____father's_____ mother.

2. My sister-in-law is my _____ wife.

3. My nephew is my _____ son.

4. My niece is my _____ daughter.

5. My aunt is my _____ sister.

6. My father-in-law is my _____ father.

7. My stepmother is my _____ second wife.

C Read the information about the family. Then, match the relationships.

Tammy Katie Jack Emma
Mike

Jack and Sylvia were married for three years. They had a boy, Mike. Jack and Sylvia got divorced. Jack remarried, and his second wife's name is Katie. Jack and Katie have two little girls, Emma and Tammy.

_b_ 1. Sylvia and Jack are   **a.** half sisters.

____ 2. Sylvia is Jack's   **b.** divorced.

____ 3. Jack has three   **c.** daughters.

____ 4. Jack has two   **d.** ex-wife.

____ 5. Emma and Tammy are Mike's   **e.** stepmother.

____ 6. Mike is Katie's   **f.** stepson.

____ 7. Katie is Mike's   **g.** children.

D Listen and write the name of the correct person.

CD 1
Track 13

Hiro
Masa Yoko Julia Loretta

Eddie Yoshiko

1. _____ Julia _____

2. _____

3. _____

4. _____

5. _____

6. _____

7. _____

Word Work	Group

Complete the information about your family in the yellow box. Share the information with your group and complete the information in the pink box.

1. I have ____ brothers.

2. I have ____ sisters.

3. I have ____ aunts.

4. I have ____ uncles.

1. Who has the most brothers? _____

2. Who has the most sisters? _____

3. Who has the most aunts? _____

4. Who has the most uncles? _____

Raising a Child

A Match the sentences with similar meanings.

  c   **1.** She's putting a clean diaper on him.

      2. She's putting on his clothes.

      3. She's giving him a bottle.

      4. She's driving him to school.

      5. She's getting him after school.

      6. She's saying good-night.

a. She's picking him up.

b. She's putting him to bed.

c. She's changing him.

d. She's feeding him.

e. She's dressing him.

f. She's dropping him off.

Grammar Connection: Object Pronouns: *him / her / them*

He's tired. I'm putting **him** to bed.
She's tired. I'm putting **her** to bed.
They're tired. I'm putting **them** to bed.

Note:
- Object pronouns take the place of a noun.
- Place an object pronoun after the verb.

B Complete the sentences with correct object pronoun: *him*, *her*, or *them*.

1. She's crying. I'm going to pick ___her___ up.

2. She needs to do her homework now. I'm going to help _____.

3. He wants to play baseball. I'm encouraging _____.

4. They're hungry. I'm going to feed _____.

5. He's upset. I'm going to rock _____.

6. It's time for the kids to go to school. I'm going to drop _____ off.

7. She has a dirty diaper. I'm going to change _____.

C Listen and write the number of each statement next to the correct request.

CD 1
Track 14

      a. Please change him.

  1   **b.** Please feed him.

      c. Please read to him.

      d. Please carry him.

      e. Please discipline him.

      f. Please put him to bed.

      g. Please drop him off.

D Write about each picture. What is each parent doing?

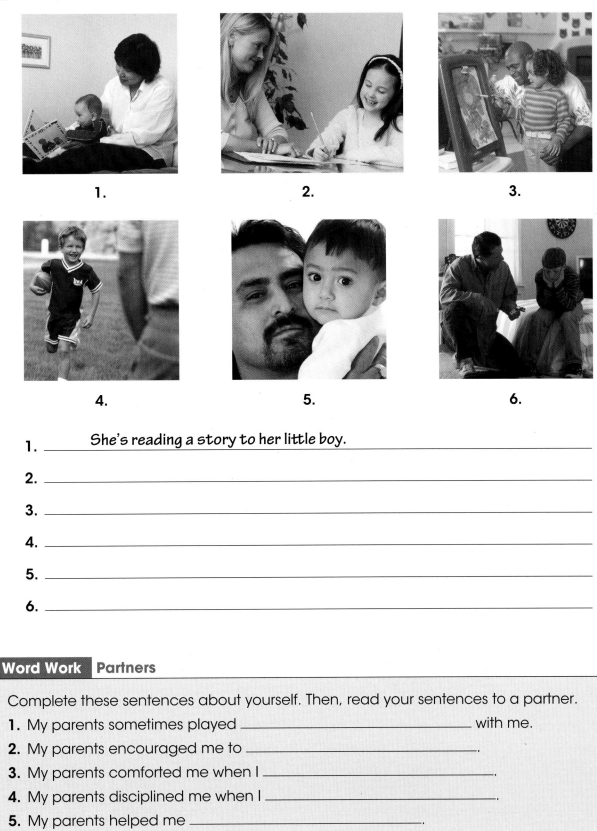

1.

2.

3.

4.

5.

6.

1. ___ She's reading a story to her little boy. _____

2. _____

3. _____

4. _____

5. _____

6. _____

Word Work **Partners**

Complete these sentences about yourself. Then, read your sentences to a partner.

1. My parents sometimes played _____ with me.

2. My parents encouraged me to _____.

3. My parents comforted me when I _____.

4. My parents disciplined me when I _____.

5. My parents helped me _____.

Life Events

A **Circle the correct verb.**

Tom [(graduated)   celebrated] from college five years ago with a degree in business. He [got   became] a job at a large accounting firm in the city. He [fell   dated] a few young women at his company, but they never became serious. For two years after college, Tom lived at home. Then, he [traveled   rented] an apartment in the city. The first day in his apartment, Tom met Kara, a young woman who lived in the apartment across the hall. They [got   fell] in love and [got   started] engaged a few months later. They [became   got] married a year later. Kara [was   had] soon pregnant and [had   got] twins the following year. Tom and Kara [had   bought] a house a few miles from the city. They need the room. Kara [is   had] pregnant again!

Grammar Connection: Past Time Clauses with *After*

> After she **got** a job, she **paid off** her college loans.
> After he **graduated** from high school, he **went** to college.

Note:
* Both the main clause and the time clause have a subject and a verb.
* Use the past tense in both the main clause and the time clause.

B **Complete the sentences about the pictures in your dictionary using the past tense.**

1. After he found a job, _____he got engaged_____.

2. After she graduated from college, _____.

3. After they got married, _____.

4. After they had a baby, _____.

5. After she retired, _____.

C **Complete the sentences. Be careful of the tense.**

1. Children _____start_____ school when they are five or six years old.

2. Marie and Joseph _____ for six months, but they didn't fall in love.

3. It is expensive to _____ a large family.

4. When Paul _____ sick, he missed two weeks of work.

5. My grandmother is going to _____ her 80th birthday on June 1st.

6. My neighbor _____ in a terrible car accident.

CD 1
Track 15

D Listen and write the number of each statement or question next to the correct event.

_____ **a.** She had a baby. _____ **e.** She is going college.

_____ **b.** They bought a house. _____ **f.** They are going to get married.

__1__ **c.** He got a job. _____ **g.** They are going to travel.

_____ **d.** He needs an operation. _____ **h.** They are going to retire.

E Read about the life of Elvis Presley. Then, complete the time line.

Elvis Presley is known as the King of Rock and Roll. He was born in Mississippi on January 8, 1935. He received his first guitar in 1946. When Elvis was 12, his family moved to Memphis, Tennessee.

Elvis began a career in music. In 1955, he signed a contract with RCA records. He soon became famous for his music, and he acted in several movies. He continued to sing, act, and give concerts for the rest of his life.

Elvis got married in 1967. He and his wife, Priscilla, had a baby in 1968 and named her Lisa Marie. In 1973, Elvis and Priscilla got divorced, and he never married again. Elvis died of heart failure on August 16, 1977.

_____1935_____	Elvis was born in Mississippi.
_____	He got a job with RCA.
_____1967_____	_____
_____1973_____	_____
_____1977_____	_____

Word Study

You already know many of the words on each vocabulary page in the dictionary. As you study, (Circle) the words that are new for you. Those are the words that you need to study.

Face and Hair

A Read the description of each woman. Write the letter of the correct picture.

a.

b.

c.

1. This woman has long blond hair. It's straight, about shoulder-length. She has long bangs. She has a friendly face. ____

2. This woman has long blond hair. Her hair is very thick and curly. She usually has braids. She has a pretty face. ____

3. This woman has long blond hair. It's straight. She doesn't have bangs. ____

Grammar Connection: Order of Adjectives

	Length / Size	Style	Color	Feature
She has	**long**	**curly**		hair.
He has a	**short**		**grey**	beard.

Note:
* Note the order of the adjectives before the noun: length / style / color

B Put the words in each sentence in the correct order.

1. curly / hair / he / short / has

He has short curly hair.

2. grey / he / beard / long / a / has

_____

3. moustache / brown has / a / long / he

_____

4. black / he / large / glasses / has

_____

5. hair / shoulder-length / has / straight / she

_____

C Write the letter(s) of the correct picture(s) next to each sentence.

a.

b.

c.

d.

e.

f.

1. He has glasses. __a__ ____ ____

2. He has curly hair. ____

3. He has straight hair. ____ ____ ____

4. His hair is gray. ____

5. He's bald. ____

6. He has a beard. ____ ____ ____

7. He has an earring. ____

8. He has a moustache. ____ ____ ____

9. He has wrinkles. ____

10. He has sideburns. ____

D Listen to each description. Write the letter of the correct man in Exercise C.

CD 1
Track 16

1. __c__   **2.** ____   **3.** ____   **4.** ____   **5.** ____

Word Work Small Group

Write the names of the students in your group. Complete the information about each student.

Name of Student	Hair Length	Hair Color	Hair Style
_____	_____	_____	_____
_____	_____	_____	_____
_____	_____	_____	_____

Daily Activities

A Look in your dictionary. Write the name of the daily activity for each item.

1. _take a coffee break_

2. _____

3. _____

4. _____

5. _____

6. _____

Grammar Connection: Simple Present Questions – Third Person

What time	does	she	get up?
Where	does	she	work?

Note:
• Put *does* after the question word.
• Use the base form of the verb in a question.

B Read the information about Marisa. Complete the questions on the next page.

Marisa

Marisa is a security guard at an airport. She gets up at 7:00 in the morning and eats breakfast. Then, she puts on her uniform and goes to work. She eats lunch at 12:00. Work finishes at 4:00. After work, Marisa goes to the gym and works out for an hour. Then, she goes home. She's tired after a long day. She goes to bed at 11:00.

1. Where _does she work_ ?   She works at an airport.

2. What _____ to work?   She wears a uniform.

3. When _____ lunch?   She eats lunch at 12:00.

4. What time _____ work?   She finishes work at 3:00.

5. Where _____ after work?   She goes to the _____.

6. How long _____?   She works out for _____.

7. What time _____ to bed?   She goes to bed at _____.

C | **Read each sentence. Check _Likely_ or _Unlikely_.**

	Likely	Unlikely
1. I go to sleep after I get dressed.	___	✓
2. I put on my makeup before I take a shower.	___	___
3. I take a nap after I get up.	___	___
4. I brush my teeth after I eat.	___	___
5. I take a shower after I take a bath.	___	___
6. I take my children to school after we eat dinner.	___	___
7. I watch TV before I go to bed.	___	___
8. I take a walk before I get up.	___	___

D | **Listen to Eric talk about his schedule. Put his day in order from 1 to 10.**

CD 1
Track 17

___ do homework   _1_ get up

___ go to gym and work out   ___ eat dinner

___ go to work   ___ eat breakfast

___ watch TV   ___ take a shower

___ get dressed for work   ___ go to bed

Word Work | **Partners**

Describe your schedules to one another. Then, write three things that are the same about your schedules.

Examples: **We both get up at 6:00 in the morning.**

If you are working alone, write a short paragraph describing your schedule.

Walk, Jump, Run

A **Look at the picture in your dictionary. Match the question and answer.**

_g_ **1.** Who's getting on the bus? **a.** the man in the blue shirt

____ **2.** Who's going up the stairs? **b.** the woman with the white and pink shirt

____ **3.** Who's leaving the building? **c.** the boy in the white and red shirt

____ **4.** Who's sitting down? **d.** the woman with the flowers on her shirt

____ **5.** Who's running? **e.** the woman in the turquoise shirt

____ **6.** Who's getting off the bus? **f.** the man in the red shirt

____ **7.** Who's getting out of the taxi? **g.** the man with the gold shirt

B **Circle the words that can follow each action.**

1. Walk: (down the stairs) over a chair (across the street)

2. Ride: a bicycle a chair a motorcycle

3. Slip: on the taxi on the ice on the banana peel

4. Leave: the meeting the classroom the street

5. Get off: the taxi the train the bus

6. Enter: the building the classroom the bicycle

7. Get out of: a car the stairs a taxi

8. Follow: the building the signs the car

Grammar Connection: Present Progressive Tense

I	am	
He	is	leaving.
We		sitting down.
You	are	
They		

Note:
* The present progressive tense tells about an action that is happening now.

C Write the opposite of each sentence.

1. They are getting on the bus.   _They are getting off the bus._

2. I am going up the stairs.   _____

3. He is entering the building.   _____

4. We are getting into the taxi.   _____

5. She is pushing the wagon.   _____

6. They are sitting down.   _____

7. I am getting in the taxi.   _____

8. He is running.   _____

CD 1
Track 18

D Listen and complete the sentences.

1. I _____leave_____ my apartment at 7:30.

2. I'm always late, so I _____ to the bus stop.

3. I _____ the bus at 14th Street.

4. The bus is always crowded in the morning, so I have to _____.

5. I _____ the bus at 53rd Street.

6. I _____ the street and _____ the building.

7. I _____ the stairs to the third floor.

8. I _____ into my classroom. I _____ and take out my books.

Word Work Pairs

Explain how you get to school. Be very specific. Write four or more sentences.

1. _I leave my . . ._ _____

2. _____

3. _____

4. _____

5. _____

Feelings

A **Match the definition and the feeling.**

_d_ **1.** worried about a future event

____ **2.** peaceful; relaxed

____ **3.** alone and feeling sad

____ **4.** containing a large amount

____ **5.** mad or upset

____ **6.** feeling sad when you are away from home

____ **7.** not interested

a. lonely

b. angry

c. full

d. nervous

e. bored

f. calm

g. homesick

Grammar Connection: *Because*

| He's nervous | **because he has** a math test today. |
| He's angry | **because she lost** her cell phone. |

Note:
- *Because* gives a reason.
- Use a subject and a verb after *because*.

B **Use the chart. Write six sentences with *because*.**

~~He's embarrassed~~		his father is in the hospital.
He's worried		he just ate two hamburgers.
He's proud	because	he's going on vacation tomorrow.
He's full		~~he broke your glass.~~
He's lonely		his son just graduated from college.
He's excited		he has no family in this country.

1. _He's embarrassed because he broke your glass._

2. _____

3. _____

4. _____

5. _____

6. _____

C Look at the Word Partnerships box on page 39 of the dictionary. Complete the sentences with *about*, *of*, or *by*.

1. I'm proud _____*of*_____ of my son. He just got his first job.

2. Are you afraid _____ dogs?

3. I'm confused _____ the directions.

4. She's angry _____ the accident. Someone ran a stop sign and hit her car.

5. He's happy _____ his work schedule. He doesn't have to work on Saturdays.

6. She's tired _____ her long drive to work.

D Listen to each situation. How does each person feel?

CD 1
Track 19

1. _____*nervous*_____

2. _____

3. _____

4. _____

5. _____

6. _____

excited
lonely
thirsty
frustrated
~~nervous~~
tired

Word Work Small Group

Look at each situation. In your notebook, write about each picture. How does each person feel? Why? Use *because* in your sentences.

1.

2.

3.

Wave, Greet, Smile

A **Complete the sentences with _to_ or _with_.**

1. I don't agree _____ with _____ you.

2. In some countries, people sometimes bow _____ each other.

3. We shook hands _____ the new employee.

4. He often argues _____ his brother about politics.

5. He danced _____ his girlfriend all night.

6. She waved _____ her neighbor.

7. She apologized _____ the boss for arriving late.

Grammar Connection: Present Time Clauses with _When_

When my brother **talks** about politics,	I always **disagree** with him.
When she **attends** a wedding,	she **dances** with her boyfriend.

Note:
* Both the main clause and the time clause have a subject and a verb.
* In a present time clause, both verbs are in the simple present tense.

B **Complete the sentences with a verb from your dictionary. Use the present tense.**

apologize	help	~~congratulate~~	comfort
invite	give	shake hands	visit

1. When a friend finds a new job, I _____ congratulate _____ him.

2. When he meets someone new, he _____ with him.

3. When a friend is sad, I _____ her.

4. When his wife has a birthday, he _____ her a gift.

5. When a friend is in the hospital, I _____ her.

6. When she hurts a friend's feelings, she _____ .

7. When they decide to have a party, they _____ their friends.

8. When her co-worker is busy, she _____ her.

C In your notebook, write about each picture. What is each person doing?

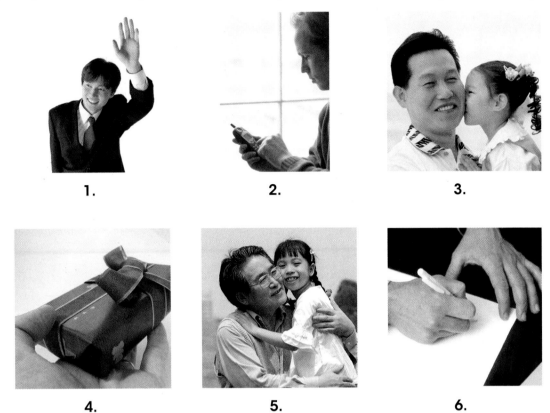

1.

2.

3.

4.

5.

6.

CD 1
Track 20

D Listen to each statement. Write the number of the correct statement next to each action.

_____ **a.** He's inviting a friend to his party.

_____ **b.** He's introducing two people.

_____ **c.** He's agreeing with a friend.

_____ **d.** He's greeting a friend.

_____ **e.** He's calling a friend.

_____ **f.** He's apologizing.

__1__ **g.** He's complimenting a friend.

Word Work Partners

Agree or disagree with these statements. Give a reason.
1. The driving age should be 18 years old.
2. Drivers should not use cell phones.
3. People should stop driving at 80 years old.
4. All drivers and passengers should wear seat belts.

Documents

A Name two documents that each person needs or will receive.

a student ID

_____

_____

_____

_____

_____

_____

_____

_____

Grammar Connection: Personal Information Questions

| **What is your** | place of birth? |
| | Social Security number? |

Note:
- When filling out a form or asking for personal information, people usually ask "What's your _____?" for each detail.

B Write the personal information question for each answer.

1. _What's your telephone number?_   555-3418

2. _____   H.

3. _____   jenny@greenhill.com

4. _____   348 Main Street

5. _____   4/21/95

6. _____   Jenny

7. _____   Smith

8. _____   143-XX-2241

C **Complete each sentence with the name of the correct form.**

1. You need a _____passport_____ to travel to Japan.

2. You need a _____ to become a teacher.

3. You need a _____ in order to apply to work.

4. A police officer will ask for your _____ and _____ if he stops you for speeding.

5. You have to apply for a _____ in order to live in another country.

6. When you finish high school, you receive a _____.

7. The first week of school, all students receive a _____.

8. Most salespeople give their _____ to customers.

9. You receive a _____ after your wedding.

10. A _____ allows a person from another country to live and work permanently in the United States.

11. An immigrant who becomes a United States citizen receives a _____.

D **Write the number of each question next to the correct answer.**

CD 1
Track 21

_____ **a.** Florida   _____ **f.** Miami

_____ **b.** Menendez   _____ **g.** 555-9847

_____ **c.** 4/21/85   __1__ **h.** 33142

_____ **d.** 15467190   _____ **i.** P.

_____ **e.** cpg22@bluebird.com   _____ **j.** Carlos

Word Work Partners

Take out two documents you have in your wallet or purse.
Discuss or list the information that each form contains.

Nationalities

A **Write three nationalities that end with these letters.**

- an	- ese	- ish
Nigerian	_____	_____
_____	_____	_____
_____	_____	_____

B **Write the nationality.**

1. Canada   Canadian   **5.** Brazil   _____

2. Chile   _____   **6.** Argentina   _____

3. Turkey   _____   **7.** Philippines   _____

4. Vietnam   _____   **8.** United States   _____

Grammar Connection: Nationalities

He is **Spanish**.
He was a famous **Spanish** artist.

Note:
- In both of these examples, *Spanish* is an adjective.

C **Guess the profession or lifework of these people. Put the nationality in the correct form. The answers are on the bottom of the next page.**

philosopher	inventor	leader	composer
~~astronaut~~	queen	artist	architect

(Russia)   **1.** Yuri Gagarin was a famous   Russian   astronaut   .

(France)   **2.** Gustave Eiffel was a famous   _____   _____ .

(India)   **3.** Mohandas Gandi was a famous _____   _____ .

(Greece)   **4.** Aristotle was a famous   _____   _____ .

(Egypt)   **5.** Cleopatra was a famous   _____   _____ .

(Italy)   **6.** Michelangelo was a famous   _____   _____ .

(United States)   **7.** Thomas Edison was a famous   _____   _____ .

(German)   **8.** Beethoven was a famous   _____   _____ .

44

D **Listen and complete each sentence with the nationality you hear.**

CD 1
Track 22

1. Hot dogs are a favorite _____ American _____ food.

2. A _____ croissant is delicious.

3. You can enjoy delicious _____ pasta in many restaurants.

4. _____ caviar is the best in the world.

5. You can order paella at the _____ restaurant in town.

6. _____ coffee is rich and flavorful.

7. Baklava is a sweet _____ dessert.

8. The new _____ restaurant has wonderful sushi.

9. Some _____ curries are mild, but others are very hot.

10. That store sells delicious _____ empanadas.

Word Work Class

Write the names of five students in your class. Write the name of each person's country and nationality.

Name	Country	Nationality
_____	_____	_____
_____	_____	_____
_____	_____	_____
_____	_____	_____
_____	_____	_____

Word Study

Write a few of your new words on an index card. Put the card in your pocket or purse. Take out the card several times a day to study the words.

Exercise C: 1. astronaut   2. architect   3. leader   4. philosopher   5. queen   6. artist   7. inventor   8. composer

Places Around Town

A Look in your dictionary. Complete the sentences.

1. The library is next to the _____courthouse_____.

2. The _____ is between the school and the motel.

3. The fire station is across from the _____.

4. The _____ is behind the college.

5. The _____ is between the stadium and the school.

6. The parking garage is next to the _____.

7. The _____ is in front of the college.

8. The _____ is in front of the church.

Grammar Connection: Future Tense – *going to*

I	am		
He	is		**visit** a friend
We		**going to**	at the hospital.
You	are		
They			

Note:
* The future tense tells about things you plan to do tomorrow, next week, or some other time in the future.

B Write six sentences using some of these cues. Give the name of the place.

buy stamps	~~see a movie~~	park my car
get some gas	pay my parking ticket	get a dog license
apply for a job	look for a good book	watch a baseball game

1. ___I'm going to see a movie at the movie theater.___

2. _____

3. _____

4. _____

5. _____

6. _____

C Write the place you can associate with these words.

1. judge, jury, lawyer _____ a courthouse_

2. doctor, operation, patient _____

3. stamp, letter, mailbox _____

4. student, teacher, test _____

5. room, bed, reservation _____

6. screen, seat, tickets _____

7. parking lot, stores, shopping bag _____

D Match the statement or question and the place.

_c_ 1. How much is this red convertible?   a. college

____ 2. We have a report of a fire on Oak Road.   b. post office

____ 3. I'd like to send this package.   c. car dealership

____ 4. The baseball score is now 5–3.   d. city hall

____ 5. Your final exam is next Monday.   e. stadium

____ 6. I need a copy of my birth certificate.   f. fire station

CD 1
Track 23

E Listen to each statement and write the letter of the correct place.

a.   b.   c.

1. _b_   2. ____   3. ____   4. ____   5. ____

6. ____   7. ____   8. ____   9. ____

Word Work | **Small Group**

Complete the sentences. Discuss your answers with your group.

1. I would like to live next to a _____.

2. I would not like to live next to a _____.

3. When I have time, I enjoy going to a _____.

Shops and Stores

A **Write the kind of store where you can buy these items.**

1. ___a clothing store___   coat   shirt   dress

2. _____   table   chair   sofa

3. _____   aspirin   toothpaste   prescription

4. _____   calendar   book   magazine

5. _____   ring   watch   necklace

6. _____   stereo   television   computer

Grammar Connection: Modal – _can_

> I **can pick up** a prescription at a drugstore.
> You **can get** a manicure at a nail salon.

Note:
• Use _can_ to show you are able to do something.

B **Complete each sentence with _can_ and the correct verb.**

wash	exercise	~~get~~	buy	order	pick up	order

1. I ____can get____ a haircut at a barbershop.

2. I _____ a birthday cake at a bakery.

3. You _____ at a health club.

4. You _____ your clean suit at a dry cleaners.

5. You _____ a hamburger at a fast food restaurant.

6. You _____ a pair of sandals at a shoe store.

7. I _____ my clothes at a laundromat.

C **Listen to a woman talk about her trip to the mall. She went to eight different stores. Where did she go first, second, third, etc.? Put the correct number in front of each store.**

CD 1
Track 24

_____ Toy store   _1_ Beauty salon   _____ Bookstore

_____ Jewelry store   _____ Pet store   _____ Clothing store

_____ Bakery   _____ Flea market

D **Write a sentence about each picture. Use the name of a store in the sentence.**

1.

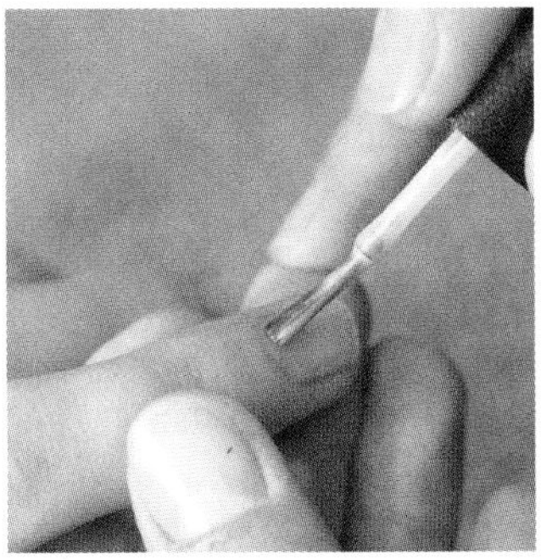

2.

3.

4.

5.

6.

1. _She is getting a manicure at a nail salon._ _____

2. _____

3. _____

4. _____

5. _____

6. _____

Word Work **Small Group**

Many stores are chain stores that sell the same items in all their locations. Name three well-known stores in each category. Talk about which stores you like.

Supermarkets: _____   _____   _____

Clothing stores: _____   _____   _____

Coffee shops: _____   _____   _____

Drugstores: _____   _____   _____

Bank

A   **Look in your dictionary. Complete the definitions.**

1. A _____loan officer_____ is a person who helps customers apply for loans.

2. A _____ is a person who keeps money in a bank.

3. A _____ is a person who watches customers carefully.

4. A _____ is a person who manages the work in a bank.

5. A _____ is a person who works at the teller window.

Grammar Connection: *I'd like to ...*

I would like to I'd like to	order new checks. make a deposit.

Note:
• *Would like* means "want."
• Use the base form of the verb after *would like to*.

B   **Read the dialogues below. Write the correct request for each response.**

> I'd like to deposit my paycheck.
> I'd like to know my balance.
> I'd like to take some money out of my account.
> ~~I'd like to rent a safe-deposit box.~~
> I'd like to buy a car, and I need to borrow some money.

1. **a:** _____I'd like to rent a safe-deposit box._____

   b: What size box do you need?

2. **a:** _____

   b: Endorse the back of the check and fill out a deposit slip.

3. **a.** _____

   b: You need to talk with a loan officer.

4. **a:** _____

   b: You need to fill out a withdrawal slip.

5. **a:** _____

   b: You have $850 in your account.

C Match.

_e_ **1.** He took money out of the bank.

_____ **2.** He put money in the bank.

_____ **3.** He signed the back of his check.

_____ **4.** He has $600 in the bank.

_____ **5.** He put his card in the ATM.

_____ **6.** He took his card from the ATM.

a. His balance is $600.

b. He endorsed his check.

c. He inserted his ATM card.

d. He deposited money.

e. He withdrew money.

f. He removed his ATM card.

CD 1
Track 25

D Listen to the information about World Bank and City Bank. Which offers better service?

	World Bank	City Bank
ATMs	_____	_____
Tellers	_____	_____
Interest on savings	_____	_____
Drive-up windows	_____	_____
Safe-deposit boxes	_____	_____

Word Work Pairs

Read the sentences and fill out the savings account passbook. Use your imagination and show two more transactions.

1. On May 4th, Ahmed opened a savings account. He made a deposit of $1,300.

2. On May 15th, Ahmed made a deposit of $400.

3. On May 23rd, Ahmed made a deposit of $200.

4. On May 30th, Ahmed received $2.35 in interest.

5. On June 6th, Ahmed made a withdrawal of $500.

6. On June 18th, Ahmed made a deposit of $800.

SAVINGS ACCOUNT

DATE	NOTE	% INTEREST	+DEPOSITS	− WITHDRAWALS	BALANCE
5/4	deposit		1,300.00		
					1,300.00

Post Office

A **Write the correct response after each question or statement.**

> Yes, there's one on the corner.   I sent it by overnight mail.
> ~~Use the stamp machine.~~   Send me a postcard.
> Did you send her a greeting card?   Put it on the scale.

1. I need some stamps.   _Use the stamp machine._

2. It's my sister's birthday.   _____

3. Is there a mailbox near here?   _____

4. How much does this package weigh?   _____

5. I'm going on vacation next week.   _____

6. How did you send the package?   _____

Grammar Connection: Adverbs of Frequency

always	95 – 100%	**sometimes**	20 – 80%
usually	80 – 99%	**rarely**	2 – 5%
often	60 – 80%	**never**	0 – 2%

Note:
- Put adverbs of frequency before the verb.
- Put adverbs of frequency after the verb *be*.
- *Sometimes* can also be used at the beginning or the end of a sentence.

B **Put the words in each sentence in order.**

1. always / I / my mailbox / check

     I always check my mailbox.

2. often / postcards / He / sends

     _____

3. to my family / sometimes / send / I / packages

     _____

4. catalogs / in their mailbox / They / sometimes / receive

     _____

5. speak / often / I / to my mail carrier

     _____

C Complete the sentences.

postage-paid	sheet	love letter	~~roll~~
postmark	bill	greeting cards	

1. A _____roll_____ of stamps has one hundred stamps.

2. A _____ of stamps has twenty stamps.

3. The telephone company sends me a _____ every month.

4. Many people send _____ to their friends on their birthdays.

5. You don't need to put a stamp on a _____ envelope.

6. Did you ever receive a _____ from your boyfriend/girlfriend?

7. The _____ shows the postage and the date sent.

D Listen to the conversations. Write the word or phrase you hear.

CD 1
Track 26

1. _____sheet of stamps_____

2. _____

3. _____

4. _____

5. _____

6. _____

7. _____

package
postcard
~~sheet of stamps~~
mailbox
mail carrier
zip code
overnight mail

Word Work   Pairs

Tell your group about each piece of mail you received yesterday.

What did you do with each piece?

What mail did you receive?

- a bill
- a letter
- a postcard
- overnight mail
- a package
- a catalog
- a greeting card

What did you do with it?

1. I opened it.
2. I looked at the _____.
3. I read it.
4. I paid the _____.
5. I threw it away.

Library

A Look at the library in your dictionary. Complete these word partnerships.

1. library _____ card _____   4. paperback _____

2. circulation _____   5. reference _____

3. online _____   6. reading _____

B Circle *T* if the statement is true. Circle *F* if the statement is false.

1. You need a library card to check out a book.   (T)   F

2. The headline in a newspaper gives the daily weather.   T   F

3. The cover of a book tells the title and the author.   T   F

4. You check out a book at the reference desk.   T   F

5. The librarian can help you find a book.   T   F

6. Look in the online catalog to find the location of a book in the library.   T   F

7. Young children enjoy looking at picture books.   T   F

Grammar Connection: Definitions

> **A dictionary** is a book of word meanings.
> **An atlas** is a book of maps.

Note:
- A definition gives the meaning of a word.

C Match the definitions. Then, write the definition of *cookbook* and *novel*.

___c___ 1. A headline is   **a.** a magazine published regularly.

_____ 2. An encyclopedia is   **b.** a book about a person's life.

_____ 3. A periodical is   **c.** the title of an article in a newspaper.

_____ 4. A biography is   **d.** a book about a person's life, written by that person.

_____ 5. An autobiography is   **e.** the name of a book or story.

_____ 6. A title is   **f.** a book giving information on many subjects.

7. A cookbook is _____

8. A novel is _____

D Circle two items you can find in each section of the library.

1. periodical section: (a newspaper) (a magazine) a biography

2. fiction section: a romance novel a dictionary a detective novel

3. reference section: a novel an atlas an encyclopedia

4. nonfiction section: a cookbook a novel an autobiography

E Where can each person look for the information he or she needs? Listen and write the number of each sentence under the correct picture.

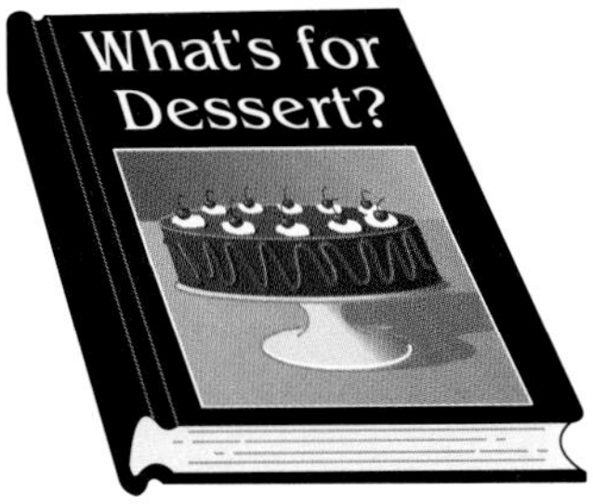

CD 1
Track 27

a. _____

b. _____

c. _____

d. _____

e. _____1_____

f. _____

Word Work Small Group

Ask your group members about the library in your area.

Name: _____ _____ _____

1. Do you have a library card? _____ _____ _____

2. How often do you go to the library? _____ _____ _____

3. What kinds of books do you like to read?_____ _____ _____

4. What newspaper do you read? _____ _____ _____

5. What is your favorite magazine? _____ _____ _____

Daycare Center

A **Complete the definitions.**

1. A bed for a baby: _____ *a crib* _____

2. A person who works in a daycare center: _____

3. The top part of a baby's bottle: _____

4. A toy that a baby shakes and it makes a noise: _____

5. A liquid food for babies: _____

6. A small compartment for coats and bags: _____

Grammar Connection: **Simple Present Tense – Third Person**

She **needs** a baby carrier.	She **doesn't need** a crib.
She **has** a crib.	She **doesn't have** a baby carrier.

Note:
• For affirmative statements, add -s or -es to the base form of the verb.
• For negative statements, use doesn't and the base form of the verb.

B **My friend is going to have a baby. She has a crib, a stroller, a changing table, and a high chair. Complete each sentence with one of these phrases:**

She needs	She doesn't have	She has	She doesn't need

1. _____ *She doesn't need* _____ a crib.

2. _____ a baby swing.

3. _____ a playpen.

4. _____ diapers and a diaper pail.

5. _____ lotion and powder.

6. _____ a stroller.

7. _____ pacifiers.

8. _____ a high chair.

C Check the correct response: *Good idea* or *Bad idea*.

		Good idea	Bad idea
1.	Put dirty diapers in a diaper pail.	✓	___
2.	Put training pants on a newborn.	___	___
3.	Put formula in a bottle.	___	___
4.	Put a bib on a toddler.	___	___
5.	Give a preschooler a bottle.	___	___
6.	Use diaper pins with a disposable diaper.	___	___
7.	Put a preschooler in a baby carrier.	___	___
8.	Show a preschooler how to share toys.	___	___

D Listen to this mother's schedule. Then, answer the questions.

CD 1
Track 28

1. What does this mother do as soon as the baby wakes up?

    She changes his diaper.

2. What does she give him after she changes his diaper?

    _____

3. Where does she put him after breakfast?

    _____

4. What does the baby do while she packs his bag?

    _____

5. What does she pack for the daycare center?

    _____

6. What doesn't she pack?

    _____

Word Work **Pairs**

You are leaving your one-year-old baby with a babysitter for the evening. Write a list of instructions that you need to give the babysitter.

Example: **Give the baby a bottle at 6:00 and again at 10:00.**

City Square

A Look at the picture in your dictionary. Circle *T* if the statement is true. Circle *F* if the statement is false.

1.	Two drivers had a traffic accident.	T	(F)
2.	The accident happened in front of the bank.	T	F
3.	A cop is directing traffic around the accident.	T	F
4.	The handicapped parking space is empty.	T	F
5.	Four pedestrians are in the crosswalk.	I	F
6.	Two people are standing at the tourist information booth.	T	F
7.	The street musician is playing a violin.	T	F
8.	There is a statue of a man on a horse in front of the art museum.	T	F
9.	The travel information booth is in front of the science museum.	T	F
10.	The fire hydrant is next to the monument.	T	F

Grammar Connection: Modals – *must / must not*

> You **must stop** at a stop sign.
> You **must not go through** a stop sign.

Note:
- Use *must* to explain rules, policies, and regulations.
- Use *must not* to show that an action is not permitted.
- Use the base form of the verb after *must* and *must not*.

B Complete the sentences with the correct modal, *must* or *must not*.

1. You _____must not_____ park next to a fire hydrant.

2. You _____ money in the parking meter.

3. You _____ report a traffic accident.

4. You _____ cross in the middle of a street.

5. You _____ obey the traffic cop.

6. You _____ stop at a stop sign.

7. You _____ cross the street in a crosswalk.

8. Cars _____ stop for pedestrians in the crosswalk.

C Look in your dictionary. How many people do you see . . .

1. in front of the art gallery? __2__

2. in the crosswalk? _____

3. sitting in front of the café? _____

4. at the street vendor? _____

5. at the newsstand? _____

6. at the tourist information booth? _____

7. looking at the traffic accident? _____

8. walking into the museum? _____

D Match the questions and answers.

__c__ 1. Why did you get a ticket?

_____ 2. Can I park here?

_____ 3. What does the billboard say?

_____ 4. Where is the newsstand?

_____ 5. Why did the driver call the cops?

_____ 6. Where can I get a map of the city?

_____ 7. Do you have money for the parking meter?

a. Keep Our City Clean!

b. Try the tourist information booth.

c. I parked in front of a hydrant.

d. He had an accident.

e. Parking is free on Sunday.

f. It's in front of the art museum.

g. No, it's a handicapped parking space.

CD 1
Track 29

E A tourist just arrived in this city. Listen and number the places he went in the correct order.

_____ the tourist information booth

_____ the café

_____ the art museum

_____ the bank

__1__ the hotel

_____ the travel agency

Word Work Small Group

How is this street scene in the dictionary the same as the street in front of your school?

Example: **There's a bank across the street from our school.**

_____

_____

How is this street scene different from the street in front of your school?

Example: **There isn't a museum on this street.**

_____

_____

Crime and Justice

A **Look in your dictionary. Complete the definitions.**

1. Starting a fire in a building: _____ *arson* _____

2. Stealing items from a store: _____

3. Selling illegal drugs: _____

4. Illegally paying money in return for favors: _____

5. Entering a house or building and stealing items: _____

B **Match the headline and the crime.**

__d__ 1. Boy Arrested for Spray Painting Bus   **a.** mugging

____ 2. Actress Charged with Taking Fur Coat from Store   **b.** murder

____ 3. Man Arrested for Killing His Brother   **c.** graffiti

____ 4. Video Shows Man with Gun Running from Bank   **d.** shoplifting

____ 5. Police Stop Street Fight   **e.** armed robbery

____ 6. Woman Hurt as Man Grabs Pocketbook   **f.** gang violence

Grammar Connection: Steal vs. Rob

She **stole** $50.	She **robbed** the bank.
She **stole** my camera.	She **robbed** the jewelry store.

Note:
- A person steals a *thing*.
- A person robs a *place*.

C **Complete the sentences with the correct verb, *stole* or *robbed*.**

1. A man _____ *robbed* _____ the bank.

2. He _____ $2,000.

3. Someone _____ my house.

4. He _____ my computer.

5. Someone _____ my car.

6. Someone _____ the gift shop.

D **Read and circle the correct words.**

Last year, Maya was the [(victim)   criminal] of a crime. A man with a knife

mugged her. A [witness   judge] saw the mugging and called the [police

lawyer]. The police made [an arrest   a trial] the same day. The next month,

there was a [trial   theft] in a [prison   courtroom]. The [police   jury]

listened to the [lawyers   murder]. They decided that the man was guilty. The

[judge   witness] sent the man to [courtroom   prison] for one year.

CD 1
Track 30

E **Listen to the description of each crime. Circle the letter of the crime.**

1. **a.** burglary   **b.** vandalism   **c.** bribery

2. **a.** drunk driving **b.** bribery   **c.** auto theft

3. **a.** burglary   **b.** vandalism   **c.** arson

4. **a.** mugging   **b.** drunk driving   **c.** drug dealing

5. **a.** arson   **b.** theft   **c.** graffiti

6. **a.** auto theft   **b.** drunk driving   **c.** mugging

Word Work **Small Group**

You are the jury. What sentence will you give for each crime?

Crime	Sentence
1. Shoplifting a pair of jeans	_____
2. Stealing a car	_____
3. Murdering a person	_____
4. Robbing a store with a gun	_____

Word Study

You will often see one of your new words in a newspaper, in a store, or on a sign.
If it's a word that you are learning, copy down the sentence or phrase.

Examples: The jury found the man guilty of armed robbery.
                   Drive-up Banking Window

Types of Homes

A Where might each person live? Write a different type of home for each picture.

1. _____a farmhouse_____

2. _____

3. _____

4. _____

5. _____

6. _____

Grammar Connection: *Used to*

I She They	**used to live**	in a villa.

Note:
- *Used to* tells about a habit or way of life in the past.
- Use the base form of the verb after *used to*.

B Complete the sentences with different types of homes.

1. My parents used to live on a _____ranch_____. Now they live in an _____apartment_____.

2. My brother used to live in a _____. Now he lives in a _____.

3. My grandmother used to live in a _____. Now she lives in a _____.

4. My sister used to live in a _____ at college. Now she lives in a _____.

5. The prince and princess used to live in a _____. Now they

   live in a _____.

6. I used to _____,

   but now I _____.

c Complete the sentences with a type of home.

1. _____A houseboat_____ is on the water.

2. _____ is a house of snow.

3. A family who lives on _____ has horses.

4. One family lives on one side of _____ and another family lives on the other side.

5. Students often live in _____.

6. People who live in _____ can move their home.

7. A family who lives in _____ usually grows corn, tomatoes, or other vegetables.

8. There are many _____ in that building. The tenants pay rent.

9. The British royal family lives in a large _____ in London.

CD 1
Track 31

D Listen to each speaker. Write the number of each statement next to the correct type of home.

___ **a.** houseboat   ___ **e.** apartment

_1_ **b.** townhouse   ___ **f.** dormitory

___ **c.** mobile home   ___ **g.** farmhouse

___ **d.** house   ___ **h.** retirement home

Word Work **Small Group**

Choose two types of homes. Write one advantage to each type of home. Write one disadvantage.

Type of home: _____

Advantage: _____

Disadvantage: _____

Type of home: _____

Advantage: _____

Disadvantage: _____

Finding a Place to Live

A Which type of housing does each statement refer to?
✔ *Apartment*, *House*, or *Both*.

	Apartment	House	Both
1. Meet the landlord.	✓	___	___
2. Apply for a loan.	___	___	___
3. Sign a lease.	___	___	___
4. Make a down payment.	___	___	___
5. Get the key.	___	___	___
6. Meet the neighbors.	___	___	___

B Complete the sentences about renting an apartment.

1. Many people _____look for_____ an apartment online.

2. In order to see the apartment, you have to _____.

3. When you see the apartment, you should _____.

4. At the time you sign the lease, you must also _____.

5. Every month, a tenant has to _____.

Grammar Connection: Present Time Clauses with *After*

After you call a realtor,	you look at many houses.
You look at many houses	after you call a realtor.

Note:
- Use a subject and a verb in both the time clause and the main clause.
- If the time clause is at the beginning of the sentence, use a comma after it.

C Combine the sentences with *after*.

1. You make an offer. You see a house you like.

   a. ___After you see a house you like, you make an offer.___

2. You buy a house. You move in.

   a. _____

3. You move in. You begin to make house payments.

   a. _____

D Wu and Ling bought a house last year. Read the paragraph and write the correct amounts below.

Wu and Ling Cho called a real estate agent last year and began looking at houses. They looked at about twenty homes and finally found one they liked. The price was $240,000. Wu and Ling made an offer of $220,000. The real estate agents negotiated the price, and the two families agreed on a price of $230,000. Wu and Ling made a down payment of $25,000, and they applied for a loan of $205,000 from a local bank. Two months later, Wu and Ling moved into their new home. Each month, they make a payment of $1,300.

The asking price of the house was ____$240,000____.

The Chos made an offer of _____.

The real estate agents negotiated a price of

_____.

The Chos made a down payment of _____.

The Chos applied for a loan for _____.

They make a house payment of _____ a month.

CD 1
Track 32

E Listen to Louis's story about renting an apartment. Put the sentences in order from 1 to 8.

_____ He paid a security deposit.

_____ He is going to pack.

_____ The landlord is going to give him the key.

__1__ He looked for an apartment.

_____ They're going to unpack.

_____ He signed the lease.

_____ They're going to arrange the furniture.

_____ They're going to load the van.

Word Work Small Group

Write three questions you should ask the landlord when you look at an apartment.

1. _____

2. _____

3. _____

Apartment Building

A Look at the apartment building in your dictionary. Match the location of each person, place, or thing.

<u>f</u> **1.** The doorman is

    2. The workout room is

    3. The courtyard is

    4. The storage area is

    5. The air conditioner is

    6. The laundry room is

    7. The peephole is

a. in the center of the building.

b. in back of the building.

c. in the door.

d. on the second floor.

e. in the basement.

f. in front of the building.

g. in the window.

Grammar Connection: Modal – *should*

> You **should pay** your rent on time.
> You **should park** in your assigned parking space.

Note:
* Use *should* to give advice or a suggestion.
* Use the base form of the verb after *should*.

B Use the cues to complete the apartment building rules.

report any problems	look through the peephole	~~use the intercom~~
speak with the doorman	lock your door	put all trash

1. You ___should use the intercom___ before you let someone into the building.

2. You _____ with the dead-bolt.

3. You _____ before you open the door.

4. If you expecting a package, you _____.

5. You _____ in the dumpster behind the building.

6. You _____ to the super.

C Read the questions. Then, write the correct answer from the box.

> There's a workout room.
> The dumpster is on the side of the building.
> Yes. And there's a door chain, too.
> Call the super.
> ~~Each apartment has one parking space.~~
> There's a laundry room.

1. Is there parking? _____ *Each apartment has one parking space.* _____

2. Where do I put the trash? _____

3. Where can I do my wash? _____

4. Is there a place to exercise? _____

5. Is there a dead-bolt on the door? _____

6. Who do I call if I have a problem? _____

CD 1
Track 33

D Listen to Sheri speak with her mother about three apartments for rent. Complete the chart as you listen.

	Size	Parking	Distance to work	Rent
1.	small studio	(Yes) No	_____	_____
2.	_____	Yes No	_____	_____
3.	_____	Yes No	_____	_____

E Which apartment do you think that Sheri should rent? Give two reasons.

_____

_____

_____

Word Work Partners

Sit with a partner. Write a conversation between a super and a person looking for an apartment to rent.

House and Garden

A Look in your dictionary. Match the item and the location.

_d_ **1.** The vegetable garden is   **a.** in the garage.

____ **2.** The rake is   **b.** on the deck.

____ **3.** The hammock is   **c.** next to the garage.

____ **4.** The trash can is   **d.** in front of the fence.

____ **5.** The grill is   **e.** on the windows.

____ **6.** The shutters are   **f.** in the backyard.

B Complete the definitions.

1. _____A skylight_____ is a window in a roof.

2. _____ tells you that someone is at the door.

3. _____ is a building for a car.

4. _____ is a door in a fence.

5. _____ is a machine used to cut grass.

Grammar Connection: Offers to Help with *I will*

I will clean the garage. **I'll** rake the leaves.	Note: • Use *I will* to make an offer to help someone. • Use the base form of the verb after *I will*.

C Write an offer to help after each statement.

fix it	open the windows	cut it
turn on the sprinkler	answer it	~~heat up the grill~~

1. It's time to start dinner. _____ *I'll heat up the grill.* _____

2. The shutter is broken. _____

3. It's hot in the house today. _____

4. The grass is high. _____

5. The garden is dry. _____

6. Someone is at the door. _____

D **Look at the picture in the dictionary. Circle the correct answer.**

1. **a.** Yes, it is.   **b.** No, it isn't.

2. **a.** Yes, it is.   **b.** No, it isn't.

3. **a.** Yes, it is.   **b.** No, it isn't.

4. **a.** Yes, they are. **b.** No, they aren't.

5. **a.** Yes, it is.   **b.** No, it isn't.

6. **a.** Yes, they are. **b.** No, they aren't.

7. **a.** Yes, it is.   **b.** No, it isn't.

E **Write the correct response after each statement.**

The lawnmower is broken.	Relax in the hammock.
I just turned on the sprinkler.	~~I'll heat up the grill.~~
I didn't hear the doorbell.	I'll open the windows.

1. It's time to start dinner. _I'll heat up the grill._

2. I'm really tired.   _____

3. It's hot in the house today. _____

4. Please cut the grass. _____

5. Please water the grass. _____

6. Is someone at the door? _____

Word Work **Partners**

In your notebook, write ten sentences about the two houses. Describe the differences.

Example: **House A has a porch, but House B doesn't.**

House A   House B

Kitchen and Dining Area

A Look at the kitchen in your dictionary. Write the correct item or place.

1. Would you like a _____glass_____ of water?

2. Please light the _____ on the table.

3. Put the yogurt in the _____ and the ice cream in the _____.

4. Please empty the _____. The dishes are clean.

5. The dishes are in the _____ above the blender.

6. The pan is very hot! Use the _____.

7. Put the banana peel in the _____, not the wastebasket.

8. Turn the _____ to 350°.

B Write the item you use to make the food in each picture.

1. _____coffeemaker_____   2. _____   3. _____   4. _____

Grammar Connection: Simple Past Tense – *Have*

When I was young, we **had** a microwave.
When I was young, we **didn't have** a microwave.

Note:
- The past tense of *have* is *had*.
- Had and *didn't have* are the same for all persons.

C Complete the sentences about yourself.

1. When I was young, we _____ a blender.

2. When I was young, we _____ a dishwasher.

3. When I was young, we _____ a coffee maker.

4. When I was young, we _____ a freezer.

5. When I was young, we _____ a garbage disposal.

D Read each statement. Check *Good idea* or *Bad idea*.

	Good idea	Bad idea
1. Put the plate in the toaster.	——	✔
2. Put the dirty dishes in the dishwasher.	——	——
3. Put the silverware in the microwave.	——	——
4. Put the bread in the toaster.	——	——
5. Put the napkins on the table.	——	——
6. Put the candles in the oven.	——	——
7. Put the glasses in the garbage disposal.	——	——
8. Put the milk in the refrigerator.	——	——
9. Put the kettle on the stove.	——	——

CD 1
Track 35

E Look at the place setting. You will hear eight statements. Write the four statements that are true.

1. _____

2. _____

3. _____

4. _____

Word Work Partners

Write or discuss: How is your kitchen similar to the kitchen in the dictionary? How is your kitchen different?

This kitchen has a table and two chairs. My kitchen has a table and four chairs.

This kitchen has a microwave. I don't need a microwave.

Living Room

A Complete the name of each item in the living room.

1. fire _____screen_____
2. smoke _____
3. throw _____
4. curtain _____
5. ceiling _____

6. coffee _____
7. house _____
8. love _____
9. rocking _____
10. wall _____

B Cross out the word that does not belong.

1.	sofa	~~wall unit~~	cushion	throw pillow
2.	curtain rod	blinds	curtain	ottoman
3.	mantel	wall	fireplace	fire screen
4.	rocking chair	sofa	vent	loveseat
5.	floor	ceiling	wall	armchair
6.	loveseat	light switch	lamp	lampshade

C Match.

___f___ 1. If you are hot,

_____ 2. If you are cold,

_____ 3. If it's too sunny,

_____ 4. If it's too dark,

_____ 5. If you are tired,

_____ 6. If you want a good book,

_____ 7. If you start a fire,

a. turn on a lamp.

b. close the blinds.

c. take a nap on the sofa.

d. start a fire.

e. put the fire screen in front of the fireplace.

f. turn on the ceiling fan.

g. look in the bookcase.

Grammar Connection: Imperatives – Giving Instructions or Directions

If you are cold, **turn up** the thermostat.
If you want to relax, **sit** in the rocking chair.

Note:
• Use the base form of the verb in an imperative sentence.

D Complete the sentences about the picture in the dictionary.

1. The _____*house plant*_____ looks dry. Please water it.

2. Sit down and put your feet on the _____.

3. Please don't smoke. The _____ will go off.

4. You can sit on the _____ and look out the window.

5. Don't put your feet on the _____.

6. Please put the book in the _____.

7. You can set the temperature in the room with the _____.

8. The television is in the_____.

9. There are two _____ in the living room, one is on the end table and one is on the mantel.

E Look at the picture of the living room and listen to the statements. Circle *T* if the statement is true. Circle *F* if the statement is false.

CD 1
Track 36

1. T (F)   6. T   F

2. T   F   7. T   F

3. T   F   8. T   F

4. T   F   9. T   F

5. T   F   10. T   F

Word Work **Partners**

The owners of this new home have a living room with a fireplace. So far, they have bought two chairs and an end table for the living room. What five items should they buy next? What colors should they choose for the items?

1. _____

2. _____

3. _____

4. _____

5. _____

Bedroom and Bathroom

A **Look at the picture in your dictionary. Write the location of each item.**

1. The mirror is _____over the dresser._____

2. The lamp is _____

3. The alarm clock is _____

4. The dresser is _____

5. The round rug is _____

6. The medicine cabinet is _____

7. The wastebasket is _____

8. The plunger is _____

9. The washcloth is _____

B **Circle the items that can complete this sentence.**

Please close the _____.

(medicine cabinet)   towel   drawer

closet   toilet seat   blanket

lamp   shower curtain   shade

Grammar Connection: Present Time Clauses with _When_

When you get up,	you make your bed.
You make your bed	when you get up.

Note:
- Use a subject and a verb in both the time clause and the main clause.
- If the time clause is at the beginning of the sentence, use a comma after the time clause.

C **Complete the sentences with a time clause.**

1. You turn on the faucet _____when you wash your hands._____

2. You close the blinds _____.

3. _____, you close the shower curtain.

4. _____, you set the alarm clock.

5. You put your head on the pillow _____.

6. _____, you look in the mirror.

D Write the correct answer after each question.

It's on the night table.	It's a king.
I like two.	No, I have a small rug.
They're blue.	~~No, it's part of the bathtub.~~

1. Do you have a separate shower? No, it's part of the bathtub.

2. What size bed do you have? _____

3. What color are your towels? _____

4. Where is your alarm clock? _____

5. Do you have a carpet on the floor? _____

6. How many pillows do you like? _____

CD 1
Track 37

E Listen to the speaker. Check if she is describing something that she likes or doesn't like about her bedroom and bathroom.

	She likes it.	She doesn't like it.
1. closet	_____	✔
2. bed	_____	_____
3. mirror	_____	_____
4. carpet	_____	_____
5. bathroom	_____	_____
6. medicine cabinet	_____	_____

Word Work Partners

Close your dictionaries. How much do you remember about the bathroom in your dictionary? Add all the bathroom items you remember to this picture.

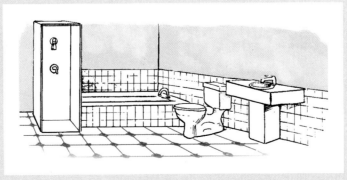

Household Problems

A Which repair person do you associate with each picture?

1. _____ 2. _____ 3. _____

B Circle two words you can use with each problem.

1. The [(toilet) (sink)   roof] is clogged.

2. The [ceiling   lightbulb   roof] leaks.

3. The [window   air conditioner   power] is broken.

4. The [power   pipe   electricity] is out.

5. The [wall   heater   light] doesn't work.

6. The [basement   bathroom   lock] is flooded.

Grammar Connection: Infinitive with *need* and *plan*

> **I need to call** a roofer.
> **I plan to call** the water company.

Note:
- We use an infinitive after some verbs in English, for example, *need* and *plan*.
- To form an infinitive, use *to* + the base form of the verb.

C Write the person each homeowner needs or plans to call.

1. He needs a new lock on his front door.   _He needs to call a locksmith._

2. She has cockroaches. _____

3. Their front window is broken. _____

4. His kitchen faucet drips. _____

5. I think our gas bill is too high. _____

6. You want a new light in the kitchen. _____

7. Her sink is clogged. _____

D Read the two problems. If the meaning is the same, write *S*. If the meaning is different, write *D*.

1. **a.** The basement is flooded.   **b.** There is water on the basement floor.   _S_

2. **a.** The power is out.   **b.** We don't have any electricity.   ___

3. **a.** The pipes are frozen.   **b.** The pipes are clogged.   ___

4. **a.** The lock is jammed.   **b.** We can't unlock the door.   ___

5. **a.** The faucet drips.   **b.** We can't turn on the water.   ___

6. **a.** The heater doesn't work.   **b.** We don't have any heat.   ___

7. **a.** The lightbulb is burned out.   **b.** The lightbulb is cracked.   ___

CD 1
Track 38

E Listen and look at the pictures of the bathroom and kitchen. If the sentence is true, circle *T*. If the sentence is false, circle *F*.

1. T (F)   3. T   F   5. T   F   7. T   F

2. T   F   4. T   F   6. T   F   8. T   F

Word Work **Partners**

Read the problems below. Check the three you think are the most serious.

☐ The lock is jammed.   ☐ The roof leaks.

☐ The power is out.   ☐ The toilet is clogged.

☐ The pipes are frozen.   ☐ The basement is flooded.

☐ The house has termites.   ☐ The house has ants.

Household Chores

A **What chores do you do? Write two chores in each group.**

I do this every day: I do this once a week: I never do this:

_____   _____   _____

_____   _____   _____

B **Circle the two words that can follow each action.**

1. wash: (the car)   (the dishes)   tho trash

2. put away: the clothes   the sink   the dishes

3. fold: the wastebasket   the clothes   the sheets

4. do: the laundry   the dishes   the rug

5. clean: the sink   the bills   the kitchen

6. polish: the rug   the furniture   the car

C **Complete the sentences with the correct verb and *it* or *them*.**

1. The wastebasket is full.	Please ___empty___ ___.	dry
2. The dishes are dirty.	Please _____ ___.	wash
3. The dirty laundry is in the basket.	Please _____ ___.	pay
4. The bills are on the desk.	Please _____ ___.	wash
5. The dishes are wet.	Please _____ ___.	fold
6. The clean clothes are in the dryer.	Please _____ ___.	mow
7. The grass is tall.	Please _____ ___.	~~empty~~
8. The lawn is dry.	Please _____ ___.	water

Grammar Connection: Object Pronouns – *it / them*

The floor is dirty.	Please mop **it**.
The floors are dirty.	Please mop **them**.

Note:
• Use an object pronoun **after** a verb.
• Use an object pronoun in place of a noun.

D This college student needs to clean his dorm room. On a piece of paper, explain what he needs to do.

Example: **There is a lot of paper in his wastebasket. He needs to empty it.**

CD 1
Track 39

E It's Saturday and Lidia and Luis cleaned today. Look at each person's *To Do* list. Listen to the speaker and check the chores they completed.

<table>
<tr><td>

Lidia - To Do

☑ clean the bedroom
☐ change the sheets
☐ do the laundry
☐ clean the bathroom
☐ scrub the toilet
☐ clean the sink
☐ mop the floor
☐ clean the kitchen
☐ cook dinner

</td><td>

Luis - To Do

☐ pay the bills
☐ empty the wastebaskets
☐ take out the trash
☐ wash the car
☐ mow the lawn
☐ vacuum the carpets
☐ polish the furniture

</td></tr>
</table>

Word Work **Partners**

Ask a partner about his/her activities last weekend. What chores did he/she do?
Circle your partner's answer.

A: **Did you do the laundry?** B: **Yes, I did. I went to the laundromat.**

1. do the laundry	Yes	No	**6.** change the sheets	Yes	No
2. cook	Yes	No	**7.** take out the trash	Yes	No
3. pay the bills	Yes	No	**8.** wash the car	Yes	No
4. dust	Yes	No	**9.** weed the garden	Yes	No
5. vacuum the carpets	Yes	No	**10.** mow the lawn	Yes	No

Cleaning Supplies

A Write the name of the cleaning item and one cleaning supply you associate with it.

1. _____sponge_____   2. _____   3. _____

___dishwashing soap___   _____   _____

B Write the word to complete each cleaning supply.

1. rubber _____gloves_____   5. paper _____

2. scrub _____   6. recycling _____

3. glass _____   7. trash _____

4. bug _____   8. scouring _____

Grammar Connection: Questions with *a / any*

Do we have	a trash bag any trash bags	for the kitchen basket?

Note:
• Use *a* for singular nouns.
• Use *any* for plural nouns and non-count nouns.

C Complete the questions with the name of a cleaning supply or item.

1. ___Do we have any dishwasher detergent___ for the dishwasher?

2. _____ for the vacuum cleaner?

3. _____ to sweep the floor?

4. _____ to clean the sink?

5. _____ to kill that mosquito?

6. _____ to polish the furniture?

7. _____ to wash the windows?

D Complete the sentences.

1. You sweep the floor with a _____broom_____ .

2. You kill flies with a _____.

3. You catch mice with a _____.

4. You wear _____ when you wash the dishes in hot water.

CD 1
Track 40

E Listen to each request. Circle the correct response.

1. **a.** Where's the vacuum cleaner?   **b.** Where's the mop?

2. **a.** Where's the dish soap?   **b.** Where's the furniture polish?

3. **a.** Where's the bug spray?   **b.** Where's the dish soap?

4. **a.** Where's the dust mop?   **b.** Where's the flyswatter?

5. **a.** Where's the squeegee?   **b.** Where's the scouring pad?

6. **a.** Where's the cleanser?   **b.** Where's the dustpan?

7. **a.** Where's the bucket?   **b.** Where's the broom?

Word Study

Put sticky notes on some of the items in your home. Look at the items several times a day and say the words out loud.

Fruits and Nuts

A Complete the sentences with the name of a fruit or nut. Some statements have many possible answers.

1. A _____ peach _____ has a large pit.

2. A _____ is the largest fruit.

3. _____ grow under the ground.

4. _____ and _____ are two kinds of berries.

5. You peel a _____.

6. An _____ and a _____ are two citrus fruits.

7. Two tropical fruits are a _____ and a _____.

8. _____ and _____ grow in my country.

9. My favorite fruit is _____.

Grammar Connection: as _____ as

| A lemon | is | **as** sour **as** | a lime. |
| A peach | is not | **as** sour **as** | a lime. |

Note:
- Use **as** _____ **as** to show that two things are the same.
- Use **not as** _____ **as** to show that two things are not the same.

B Use the adjectives in the word box to complete the sentences about the fruits and nuts. Use *as* _____ *as* or *not as* _____ *as*.

1. A pear is _____ as juicy as _____ a plum.

2. An orange is _____ a grapefruit.

3. Cherries are _____ strawberries.

4. A coconut is _____ a watermelon.

5. Walnuts are _____ pecans.

6. A mango is _____ a papaya.

7. This apricot is _____ this mango.

8. This watermelon is _____ this cantaloupe.

| healthy |
| delicious |
| fresh |
| expensive |
| sweet |
| cheap |
| ripe |
| juicy |

C Circle the two words that can follow each word or expression.

1. Canned: lemons (peaches) (pears)

2. Dried: apples cantaloupe bananas

3. Juicy: avocados oranges plums

4. Peel a: mango strawberry banana

D Write the names of the fruit in the produce section of the farmers' market.

Lemons 50¢

CD 1
Track 41

E Listen as the two workers put today's prices on the fruit at the farmers' market in Exercise D. Write the price of each fruit.

Word Work **Partners**

You are making a fruit salad for your family. Write the recipe.

_____

_____

_____

_____

_____

_____

83

Vegetables

A Write the name of each vegetable.

1. _____ 2. _____ 3. _____ 4. _____

5. _____ 6. _____ 7. _____ 8. _____

Grammar Connection: Count and Non-count Nouns

Count Nouns	Non-count Nouns
We have **a potato**. We have **some potatoes**.	We have **some lettuce**.
We don't have **a potato**. We don't have **any potatoes**.	We don't have **any lettuce**.

Note:
- Count nouns are items we can count. They can be singular or plural.
- Non-count nouns are items we cannot count. Do not use *a* with non-count nouns. Do not use the plural *s* with non-count nouns.
- Use *any* for the negative with plural count nouns and with non-count nouns.

B Circle the correct word.

1. We need (a, an, (some), any) carrots and (a, an, some, any) celery.

2. Don't buy any (a, an, some, any) peas. We have (a, an, some, any).

3. We have (a, an, some, any) bell pepper. We need (a, an, some, any) eggplant.

4. We don't need (a, an, some, any) cabbage.

5. Please get (a, an, some, any) chickpeas when you are at the store.

6. We need (a, an, some, any) lettuce and (a, an, some, any) tomato for the salad.

7. I need (a, an, some, any) chickpeas and (a, an, some, any) celery for this recipe.

C **Read the description. Write the name of the correct vegetable from Exercise A.**

1. These small, red vegetables are good in salads and soups. In many countries, people cook them with onions and other seasonings. ___kidney beans___

2. People make pasta sauce with this red vegetable. _____

3. This small vegetable is flavorful and gives a strong taste to sauces, soups, and other foods. _____

4. This green vegetable is the main ingredient in many salads. _____

5. This popular vegetable can be baked, boiled, mashed, or french fried.

    _____

6. This long, orange vegetable grows under the ground. _____

CD 1
Track 42

D **Listen to two friends plan a salad for dinner. Circle the items they will include in the salad.**

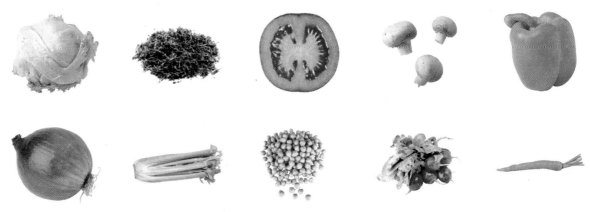

Word Work **Partners**

Start with lettuce. What other vegetables do you like in a salad? Write a salad recipe with vegetables you both like.

_____

_____

_____

_____

_____

Meat, Poultry, and Seafood

A Unscramble each word. Write the kind or cut of meat.

1. laasmi _____salami_____   **4** ahm _____

2. segl _____   **5.** gsinw _____

3. brsi _____   **6.** sssgaaeu _____

B Complete the crossword puzzle.

Across

3

6

7

8

```
                              1
                    2         3
                              c  r  a  b
          4                              5
                              6
          7                   
                              8
```

Down

1    2   4   5

Grammar Connection: Count and Non-count Nouns with Quantity

Count Nouns	Non-count Nouns
We have a pork chop.	
We have **some** pork chops.	We have **some** ham.
We have **a few** pork chops.	We have **a little** ham.
We have **a lot of** pork chops.	We have **a lot of** ham.
We don't have **any** pork chops.	We don't have **any** ham.

Note:
- For count nouns, use *some*, *a few*, or *a lot of* for quantity.
- For non-count nouns, use *some*, *a little*, or *a lot of* for quantity.
- For the negative, use *any* for quantity.

C Complete the sentences with the correct quantity. Answers may vary.

1. We don't have ____any____ salmon in the freezer.

2. We only have _____ hot dogs, so we need more.

3. Please buy _____ chicken breasts. We have ten people coming for dinner!

4. The fish store doesn't have _____ swordfish today.

5. Please don't buy _____ steak. We had steak last night.

6. For the party, we don't need _____ chicken wings.

7. I'd like a ham sandwich for lunch. Please buy _____.

8. We had _____ pork roast for dinner last night.

D Complete the sentences with a kind of meat, poultry, or seafood.

1. I have never tried _____.

2. How do you like your steak? I like it _____.

3. At times, it's difficult to find _____ in the supermarket.

4. Lean meat is healthier for you than _____ meat.

5. Seafood is healthier than _____ because it contains very little fat.

6. _____ is my favorite meat.

E Complete the sentences with the meat, poultry, or seafood you hear.

CD 1
Track 43

1. We're having _____ francése tonight.

2. The special tonight is _____.

3. I'd like a _____ sandwich.

4. A _____ sandwich, please.

5. We're having _____ for dinner tonight.

6. I'll cook some _____ on the grill.

7. I'm going to make meatballs with this _____.

8. The _____ in that restaurant are delicious.

9. My brother is a fisherman. He often brings home fresh _____.

Word Work Partners

Which kind of meat, poultry, or seafood do you like best? Compare your answers with your partner.

1. I like _____ salad. 3. I like _____ soup.

2. I like _____ sandwiches. 4. I like _____ on the grill.

Inside the Refrigerator

A Complete the sentences.

1. I sometimes eat _____ for breakfast.

2. When I'm thirsty, I like to drink _____.

3. _____ is good for dessert.

4. I put _____ on my salad.

5. I put _____ on waffles.

6. I like _____ eggs.

7. I like _____ cheese.

8. I sometimes have _____ salad for dinner.

9. I have never eaten _____.

Grammar Connection: *Is there / Are there* Questions

Is there a cake		Yes, there is.	No, there isn't.
Are there any eggs	in the refrigerator?	Yes, there are.	No, there aren't.
Is there any salad		Yes, there is.	No, there isn't.

Note:
- Use *Is there a/an* with singular count nouns.
- Use *Are there any* with plural count nouns.
- Use *Is there any* with non-count nouns.

B Complete the questions and answers about the refrigerator in your dictionary.

1. ___Is there any___ milk in the refrigerator?   ___Yes, there is.___

2. _____ jam in the refrigerator?   _____

3. _____ grapes in the refrigerator?   _____

4. _____ tuna in the refrigerator?   _____

5. _____ butter in the refrigerator?   _____

6. _____ salad in the refrigerator?   _____

7. _____ waffles in the freezer?   _____

8. _____ cold cuts in the refrigerator?   _____

C Match the question and answer.

_c_ 1. What kind of soda do you drink?

_____ 2. What kind of ice cream do you like?

_____ 3. What kind of cold cuts do you like?

_____ 4. What kind of cheese do you buy?

_____ 5. What kind of salad dressing do you buy?

_____ 6. What kind of jam do you buy?

_____ 7. What kind of frozen vegetables do you buy?

_____ 8. What kind of milk do you drink?

a. ham and roast beef

b. cheddar

c. cola

d. grape and strawberry

e. vanilla

f. skim

g. peas and green beans

h. Italian

CD 1
Track 44

D Listen to this couple write a list of items they need to buy at the supermarket. Check *Buy* or *Don't buy*.

	Buy	Don't buy			Buy	Don't buy
1. mayonnaise	✓	_____	6. salad dressing		_____	_____
2. yogurt	_____	✓	7. milk		_____	_____
3. eggs	_____	_____	8. jam		_____	_____
4. syrup	_____	_____	9. ice cream		_____	_____
5. cheese	_____	_____				

E Draw a line from each item to the correct label of ingredients.

mayonnaise ——— Oil, eggs, vinegar, salt, sugar, lemon juice

ketchup   Milk, sugar, strawberries

dressing   Tomatoes, vinegar, corn syrup, salt, spices

yogurt   Water, vinegar, oil, sugar, seasonings

Word Work Partners

Circle the items you have in your refrigerator. Write the names of three more items in your refrigerator.

milk	cheese	tofu	_____
eggs	mayonnaise	cold cuts	_____
yogurt	soda	butter	_____

Food to Go

A Complete the sentences about the calories and fat in these foods.

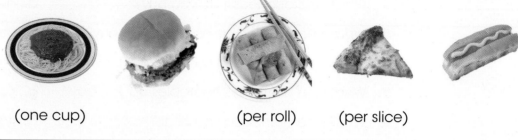

	(one cup)		(per roll)	(per slice)	
Calories:	140	440	300	290	310
Fat (mg):	5	21	11	10	18

1. A hamburger has _____440_____ calories.

2. Two slices of pizza have _____ calories.

3. Two egg rolls have _____ calories.

4. A hamburger has _____ mg of fat.

5. Two cups of spaghetti have _____ mg of fat.

6. A slice of pizza has more calories than _____.

7. A hot dog has less fat than _____.

8. The healthiest choice for lunch is _____.

Grammar Connection: Past Statements with *but*

> I **ordered** two slices of pizza, **but** you only gave me **one**.
> I **ordered chicken** teriyaki, but you **gave** me **beef** teriyaki.

Note:
• Use *but* to show a contrast in ideas.

B Complete the sentences with fast food from your dictionary.

1. I asked for a doughnut, but you gave me ____*a muffin*____.

2. I ordered coffee, but you gave me _____.

3. I asked for ketchup on my hamburger, but you put _____ on it.

4. I wanted steamed rice, but you gave me _____.

5. I ordered a burrito, but you gave me _____.

6. I ordered black beans, but you gave me _____.

7. I wanted lasagna, but you gave me _____.

C Look at the menu. Figure out the cost of each order below.

Debbie's Diner			
Hamburger	$5.00	Muffin	$2.00
Hot Dog	$3.00	Donut	$1.25
Fish and Chips	$8.00	Bagel	$1.50
Chicken Sandwich	$6.00	Coffee	$1.00
Ham Sandwich	$6.50	Tea	$1.00
French Fries	$2.00	Soda	$1.25

1. _____   **2.** _____   **3.** _____

CD 1
Track 45

D Listen to each question. Circle the letter of the correct response.

1. (**a.**) black   **b.** a tortilla   **5. a.** soy sauce   **b.** tea

2. a. ketchup   **b.** a straw   **6. a.** chopsticks   **b.** french fries

3. a. medium   **b.** salsa   **7. a.** salsa   **b.** a burrito

4. a. fried   **b.** large   **8. a.** large   **b.** baked

Word Work | **Small Group**

Discuss or write the answers.

1. What fast food restaurants are in this area?

2. How often do you eat at a fast food restaurant?

3. What is your favorite fast food restaurant?

4. What do you usually order there?

Cooking

A **Write a food that you prepare each way.**

1. I grill _____.

2. I roast _____.

3. I microwave _____.

4. I marinate _____.

5. I bake _____.

6. I steam _____.

7. I simmer _____.

8. I broil _____.

Grammar Connection: Imperative for Directions

> **Measure** 2 cups of flour.
> **Chop** 1 small onion.

Note:
* Use the base form of the verb to give directions.

B **Complete the sentences.**

Grate	Grease	Puree	Simmer
Roast	~~Season~~	Sauté	Slice

1. _____Season_____ the chicken with salt and pepper.

2. _____ the onions with a sharp knife.

3. _____ the turkey for three hours at 350°.

4. _____ the soup for two hours.

5. _____ the onions and peppers in oil in a frying pan.

6. _____ the strawberries, milk, and yogurt in a blender.

7. _____ 1/2 cup of cheddar cheese.

8. _____ two cake pans.

C **Read the directions. Check *Possible* or *Not possible*.**

	Possible	Not possible
1. Peel the lettuce.	____	✓
2. Bake the cake.	____	____
3. Boil the cookies.	____	____
4. Slice the tomato.	____	____

	Possible	Not possible
5. Sift the strawberries.	____	____
6. Scramble the eggs.	____	____
7. Measure the flour.	____	____

D **Circle the correct directions in the recipe.**

Blueberry Banana Pancakes

2 cups pancake mix	2 eggs
1 large banana	3 tablespoons oil
1 3/4 cups milk	1 cup blueberries

(Grease   Season) a large frying pan. (Marinate   Puree) the banana in a blender for 30 seconds. (Cook   Add) the eggs, milk, and oil and puree for 30 more seconds. Put the pancake mix into a large bowl. (Whisk   Peel) the wet and dry ingredients together. Gently (sift   stir) in the blueberries. (Cook   Roast) the pancakes for one to two minutes on each side. Top the pancakes with more blueberries.

CD 1
Track 46

E **Listen and complete the recipe.**

Chili

1 onion	2 teaspoons cumin
1 tablespoon olive oil	1 1/2 cups of crushed tomatoes
1 pound ground beef	1 15-ounce can kidney beans
2 tablespoons chili powder	

1. ____Chop____ the onion. _____ in olive oil for five minutes.

2. _____ the ground beef and _____ for five more minutes.

3. _____ the chili powder and cumin.

4. _____ in the tomatoes and beans. _____ for twenty minutes.

Word Work **Small Group**

People prepare rice many different ways. Write or explain one of your family's favorite recipes with rice.

Cooking Equipment

A **Look in your dictionary. Check the location of each item.**

	on the wall	on a shelf	on the island	on the stove
hand mixer	___	___	✓	___
mixing bowl	___	___	___	___
wok	___	___	___	___
grill	___	___	___	___
cake pan	___	___	___	___
frying pan	___	___	___	___
casserole	___	___	___	___

Grammar Connection: *To* for Purpose

> You use a can opener **to open** a can.
> You use a spatula **to turn** hamburgers.

Note:
- *To* expresses purpose.
- Use the base form of the verb after *to*.

B **Write a purpose for each kitchen equipment item.**

1. You use a colander _____to drain pasta_____.

2. Use a whisk _____.

3. You use a meat thermometer _____.

4. Use a mixer _____.

5. Use a food processor _____.

6. You use a wok _____.

7. Use a grater _____.

8. You use a ladle _____.

C Look in your dictionary. Complete the names of the cooking equipment.

1. a cutting _____   5. a cookie _____
2. a vegetable _____   6. a cake _____
3. _____ cups   7. a set of _____
4. a can _____   8. a mixing _____

D Write four items from your dictionary in each group.

I use this item every day.   I use this item once a week.   I seldom use this item.

_____   _____   _____

_____   _____   _____

_____   _____   _____

_____   _____   _____

CD 1
Track 47

E Listen to each statement. Write the number of the correct item under each picture.

a.   b.   c.   d.

_____   _____   _____

e.   f.   g.   h.

_____   1   _____

Word work Small Group

You are making the following items. List the cooking equipment you will need.

A cake: _____

_____

Scrambled eggs: _____

_____

Measurements and Containers

A Write the word for each item. Use a measure or container.

1. a bunch of bananas

2. _____

3. _____

4. _____

5. _____

6. _____

Grammar Connection: Containers

| How much is the hand cream? | **A tube** of hand cream is $6.00. |
| How much are the cherries? | **A pound** of cherries is $3.00. |

Note:
- When we talk about quantity, we often need to use measurement or container words.

B Answer the questions. Use a measurement or container to give a price. There are several possible correct answers.

1. How much is the olive oil? _A bottle of olive oil is $10.00._

2. How much are the potatoes? _____

3. How much are the cookies? _____

4. How much is the yogurt? _____

5. How much are the flowers? _____

6. How much are the carrots? _____

7. How much are the eggs? _____

8. How much is the soap? _____

C Complete the sentences with a container. There are several correct answers.

1. We don't have any milk.   _I'll buy a quart._

2. We don't have any soup.   _____

3. We don't have any blueberries.   _____

4. We don't have any bread.   _____

5. We don't have any rice.   _____

6. We don't have any apple juice.   _____

7. We don't have any mayonnaise.   _____

D Circle the amount that is larger.

1. **a.** one teaspoon   (**b.**) one tablespoon

2. **a.** one cup   **b.** one tablespoon

3. **a.** one pint   **b.** one cup

4. **a.** one cup   **b.** one quart

5. **a.** one quart   **b.** one ounce

6. **a.** one gallon   **b.** one quart

7. **a.** one cup   **b.** one liter

CD 1
Track 48

E Listen to each question. Circle the amount each person should buy.

1. (**a.**) one quart   **b.** one basket   5. **a.** one loaf   **b.** one jar

2. **a.** two bunches   **b.** two bars   6. **a.** one six-pack   **b.** one tray

3. **a.** one bag   **b.** one bottle   7. **a.** one piece   **b.** one carton

4. **a.** two pots   **b.** two pounds   8. **a.** four crates   **b.** four containers

Word Work **Partners**

How much of each item do you usually buy each week?
Who buys more of each item?

1. milk   **3.** bread   **5.** eggs

2. soda   **4.** juice   **6.** rice

Supermarket

A Look at the picture of the supermarket in your dictionary.
Circle *T* if the statement is true. Circle *F* if the statement is false.

1. There are six aisles in the supermarket.   T   (F)

2. The deli counter is on the right.   T   F

3. There is a scale on the deli counter.   T   F

4. The produce department is in the back.   T   F

5. Six customers are using shopping carts.   T   F

6. The three cashiers are busy.   T   F

7. The bagger is putting the groceries in a plastic bag.   T   F

Grammar Connection: Questions and Answers with *or*

Did he use a shopping cart **or** a basket?	He used a shopping cart.
	He used a shopping basket.

Note:
• Be careful when you answer an *or* question! Do not give a *Yes* or *No* answer.

B Answer the *or* questions about a supermarket.

1. Did she stop at the bakery or at the deli counter?

   She stopped at the deli counter.

2. Do you ask for paper bags or plastic bags?

   _____

3. Did they buy pretzels or potato chips?

   _____

4. Is milk in the beverage section or the dairy section?

   _____

5. Can you find napkins in the paper goods section or the household cleaners section?

   _____

6. Is he a checker or a bagger?

   _____

C Add one more item to each section of a supermarket.

1. canned goods: soup   _____
2. dairy products: yogurt   _____
3. frozen foods: ice cream   _____
4. bakery: cake   _____
5. deli counter: potato salad _____

D Put the steps in order.

_____ The customer pays the cashier.

__1__ The customer takes a shopping cart.

_____ The bagger puts the groceries in plastic or paper bags.

_____ The customer walks up and down the aisles and shops for groceries.

_____ The customer goes to the checkout counter.

_____ The cashier uses a barcode scanner to total the groceries.

E Listen to a customer ask about the location of each item. Circle the letter of the correct section.

CD 1
Track 49

1. (a.) pet food   b. beverages   c. bakery
2. a. canned goods   b. paper products   c. deli counter
3. a. dairy products   b. frozen foods   c. household cleaners
4. a. paper products   b. canned goods   c. deli counter
5. a. produce   b. dairy products   c. meats and poultry
6. a. pet food   b. beverages   c. meats and poultry
7. a. produce   b. canned goods   c. paper products
8. a. deli counter   b. bakery   c. frozen foods

Word Work Small Group

Discuss or write the answers.
1. How often do you go to the supermarket?
2. Which supermarket do you usually shop at?
3. Does it have a good produce section?
4. Does it have a bakery?
5. What kind of snacks do you sometimes buy?
6. Does the supermarket have barcode scanners at the checkout counters?

Restaurant

A Look in your dictionary. Write each word in the correct group.

bowl	~~appetizer~~	dessert	waiter
waitress	glass	main course	cup
plate	busser	chef	salad

The Meal	**People**	**Dishes**
appetizer		

Grammar Connection: *Be supposed to*

I	am		
He She	**is**	**supposed to** **not supposed to**	**clean** the tables. **bring** the check. **wear** an apron.
We You They	**are**		

Note:
* Use *be supposed to* express expectations or requirements.
* Use the base form of the verb after *be supposed to*.

B Complete these sentences about working in a restaurant. Use the verb in parentheses with *be supposed to*.

1. The server (put) _____ is supposed to put _____ fresh flowers on each table.

2. The waitresses (wear) _____ are not supposed to wear _____ heels.

3. I (give) _____ the menu to the woman first, then the man.

4. The waiter (take) _____ the beverage order first.

5. I (bring) _____ the main course when the customer is still eating an appetizer.

6. The waiter (refill) _____ the water glass when it is low.

7. We (check) _____ the salad bar every ten minutes.

8. The waitress (bring) _____ the check when the customer is still eating.

CD 1
Track 50

C **Listen and write the name of the item that each customer is requesting.**

1. _____high chair_____

2. _____

3. _____

4. _____

5. _____

6. _____

7. _____

8. _____

9. _____

10. _____

Word Work   Partners

Put the restaurant items in pairs. Explain why the items belong together.

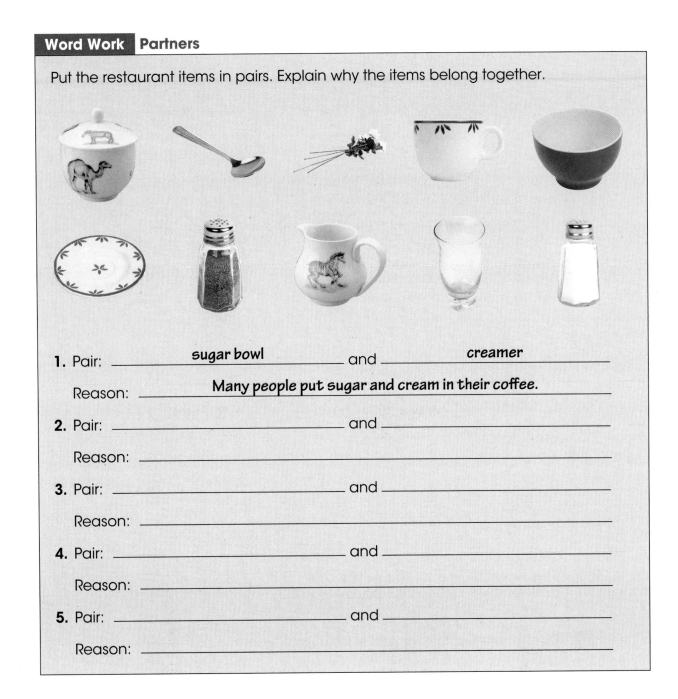

1. Pair: _____sugar bowl_____ and _____creamer_____

   Reason: _____Many people put sugar and cream in their coffee._____

2. Pair: _____ and _____

   Reason: _____

3. Pair: _____ and _____

   Reason: _____

4. Pair: _____ and _____

   Reason: _____

5. Pair: _____ and _____

   Reason: _____

Order, Eat, Pay

A Read the quote. What did each person do at the restaurant?

1. "The food is delicious."   _He complimented the chef._

2. "I left the waiter $10."   _____

3. "I'd like a table for two for 7:00."   _____

4. "I'd like the check, please."   _____

5. "Here's my credit card."   _____

6. "I'd like a salad and steak."   _____

7. "A piece of cake and two forks, please." _____

Grammar Connection: Past Questions

Where	did	they	make a reservation?
When	did	he	clear the table?
	Did	they	thank the server?

Note:
• Put *did* after the question word.
• Use the base form of the verb in a question.

B Write the question for each response.

1. What _____ _did she order_ _____? She ordered lasagna.

2. What _____? She drank iced tea.

3. How many _____? He waited on ten people.

4. _____ Yes, they enjoyed their meal.

5. _____ Yes, they shared a dessert.

6. When _____ They paid the check after they had
   _____? coffee.

7. How _____? He paid with a credit card.

8. How much _____? He left a $10 tip.

C Circle two words that can follow each verb.

1. pour: (water)   a meal   (coffee)

2. serve: a meal   a dessert   a tip

3. compliment: the waiter   the cook   the check

4. spill: a reservation   a drink   coffee

5. ask for: the check   a menu   a customer

6. refill: the water   the coffee   the table

CD 1
Track 51

D **Listen to the story of Luis's first night as a waiter. Then, read each statement and circle *True* or *False*.**

1. Mr. and Mrs. Park made a reservation at the restaurant.	(True)	False
2. Luis waited on Mr. and Mrs. Park.	True	False
3. Mr. Park ordered a large pizza with sausage.	True	False
4. Luis spilled water on the table.	True	False
5. Mr. Park complimented the waiter.	True	False
6. The manager thanked the server.	True	False
7. Mr. Park paid the check.	True	False
8. Mr. Park left a big tip for Luis.	True	False

Word Work | Small Group

Discuss or write the answers.

1. How often do you eat out?
2. What kind of food do you like?
3. What is your favorite restaurant in this area?
4. How is the service?
5. Do you sometimes share a salad or dessert?
6. Did you ever take home a doggie bag?
7. How much tip do you leave for the server?

Word Study

It is normal to try to translate new words into your first language. After you hear a word a few times, form a relationship between the word and the picture in your mind. For example, after you learn the word "vase," don't continue to translate the word. Try to see a picture of a vase with flowers in it.

Clothes

A Circle the clothes people wear when it's cold outside.

(a sweater) a jacket a T-shirt a hat shorts

a gown a scarf a trench coat a shawl a poncho

B Circle the correct word.

1. When it's raining, I wear a [(raincoat) tie].

2. When I exercise, I wear a sweatshirt and [a skirt sweatpants].

3. A police officer wears a [blouse uniform] to work.

4. Wear a blue [sari tie] with that shirt.

5. When it is windy, I wear a [vest windbreaker].

6. Many people wear [hats ponchos] to protect their skin from the hot sun.

7. It's going to be a formal party. You should wear [a dress jeans].

Grammar Connection: *So*

| My aunt is pregnant, | **so she is wearing a maternity dress.** |
| I'm exercising, | **so I'm wearing shorts and a T-shirt.** |

Note:
- Use *so* to show a result or logical conclusion.
- Use a subject and a verb after *so*.

C Complete each sentence with the clothes the person is wearing.

1. It's raining, so the children ___are wearing raincoats___.

2. It's cold outside, so he _____.

3. Jack has a job interview, so he _____.

4. It's hot today, so I _____.

5. My sister is getting married, so she _____.

6. Avery is going to work, so she _____.

7. I'm going to school, so I _____.

D **Read each statement. Check *Good idea* or *Bad idea*.**

	Good idea	Bad idea
1. It's raining, so I'm wearing a raincoat.	✓	___
2. It's cold, so I'm wearing shorts.	___	___
3. It's hot, so I'm wearing a T-shirt.	___	___
4. My brother is getting married, so he's wearing blue jeans.	___	___
5. I'm exercising, so I'm wearing a suit.	___	___
6. My aunt is pregnant, so she's wearing a maternity dress.	___	___
7. I'm going to work, so I'm wearing my uniform.	___	___
8. I have a job interview, so I'm wearing sweatpants.	___	___
9. I'm riding a bike, so I'm wearing a skirt.	___	___
10. My sister is getting married, so she's wearing a gown.	___	___

CD 2
Track 1

E **Listen to each speaker. Number the two items each person bought.**

a. _____   b. _____   c. _____   d. _____   e. __1__

f. _____   g. _____   h. _____   i. __1__   j. _____

Word Work   **Small Group**

Discuss or write the answers in your notebook.
1. What clothing stores do you shop at?
2. When is the last time you went to a clothing store?
3. What did you buy?
4. How much money did you spend?

Sleepwear, Underwear, and Swimwear

A Circle the items that come in pairs.

socks   slip   camisole   boxer shorts   nylons

swimsuit   panties   stockings   tank top   tights

B Look at the clothesline in the dictionary. Answer the questions.

1. What color is the T-shirt?   It's white.

2. What color are the flip flops?   _____

3. What color is the leotard?   _____

4. What color are the briefs?   _____

5. What color are the slippers?   _____

6. What color is the bathrobe?   _____

7. What color is the slip?   _____

8. What color are the pajamas?   _____

Grammar Connection: Questions with *How much*

How much **is this slip**?	It's $18.
How much **is this pair of socks**?	It's $5.
How much **are these socks**?	They're $5.

Note:
- Use *this* for a singular item and for a pair.
- Use *these* for plural items.

C Complete the questions. Ask about the price of each item.

1. _____How much is this_____ pair of slippers?   It's $14.

2. _____ nightgown?   It's $23.

3. _____ pajamas?   They're $11.

4. _____ pair of pantyhose?   It's $7.

5. _____ trunks?   They're $19.

6. _____ pair of tights?   It's $8.

7. _____ camisole?   It's $18.

8. _____ panties?   They're $6.

D Complete the sentences.

1. Women wear a _____slip_____ under a dress.

2. Men usually wear a _____ under a dress shirt.

3. Dancers usually wear a _____ and _____.

4. Men usually sleep in _____.

5. Women usually sleep in a _____ or _____.

6. People wear _____ with their sneakers.

7. When it's very cold, people who work outside often wear _____ under their clothes.

E Match the questions and answers.

_c_ 1. Do you wear tights?   a. No, I wear a nightshirt.

___ 2. Do you wear a bikini?   b. No, I wear boxers.

___ 3. Do you wear slippers at the beach?   c. No, I wear pantyhose.

___ 4. Do you wear briefs?   d. No, I wear an undershirt.

___ 5. Do you wear pajamas?   e. No, I wear flip flops.

___ 6. Do you wear a tank top under a dress shirt?   f. No, I wear a bathing suit.

F Listen and write the correct price under each item.

CD 2
Track 2

a. $ _____   b. $ 23 _____   c. $ _____   d. $ _____

e. $ _____   f. $ _____   g. $ _____   h. $ _____

Word Work Partners

Look in your dictionary. Make a list of five items that you can put in the dryer.

Make a list of five items that you should hang on a clothesline.

Shoes and Accessories

A Write the names of eight accessories that this woman is wearing or carrying.

1. _____ring_____
2. _____
3. _____
4. _____
5. _____
6. _____
7. _____
8. _____

B Write the names of eight items that come in pairs.

1. a pair of _____sandals_____
2. a pair of _____
3. a pair of _____
4. a pair of _____
5. a pair of _____
6. a pair of _____
7. a pair of _____
8. a pair of _____

Grammar Connection: Modal – *should*

For a day at the beach, you **should wear** sandals.

Note:
- Use *should* to give advice or a suggestion.
- Use the base form of the verb after *should*.

C Tell each person what kind of shoes to wear for each occasion.

1. For a hike in the mountains, you ___*should wear hiking boots.*___
2. For a day at the beach, you _____
3. For a formal party, a woman _____
4. For a run in the park, you _____
5. When it's snowing outside, the children _____
6. With a business suit, a man _____
7. With a business suit, a woman _____

D Complete the sentences.

1. I stand all day at work, so I wear ___comfortable___ shoes.

2. When James asked Kathy to marry him, he gave her a _____.

3. What time is it? I can't find my _____.

4. It's cold outside. You should wear your _____ and your

   _____.

5. I don't have pierced ears, so I don't have to wear _____.

6. My dad doesn't like belts, so he wears _____.

7. It's going to be sunny at the beach today. Wear your _____.

8. A businessman or businesswoman carries papers in a _____.

CD 2
Track 3

E Listen to the conversation between a mother and her daughter. Match the item and the location.

___b___ 1. pumps   **a.** in her purse

_____ 2. hat and gloves   **b.** in a bag in the car

_____ 3. purse   **c.** next to the TV

_____ 4. wallet   **d.** in the car

_____ 5. briefcase   **e.** on the table

_____ 6. sunglasses   **f.** in her coat pocket

_____ 7. key chain   **g.** on the desk

Word Work **Partners**

Dress up this young man. Draw and label
the shoes and accessories he is wearing.

Describing Clothes

A Match the clothes and the statement.

     a.   **b.**   **c.**   **d.**   **e.**

1. She's wearing a straight skirt. _b_

2. She's wearing a pleated skirt. ____

3. She's wearing a long skirt. ____

4. She's wearing a tight skirt. ____

5. She's wearing a short skirt. ____

6. She's wearing a cardigan sweater. ____

7. She's wearing a polo shirt. ____

8. She's wearing a turtleneck sweater. ____

9. She's wearing a crew neck sweater. ____

10. She's wearing a V-neck sweater. ____

B Write a response for each question, beginning with *No*.

1. Should I wear a pleated skirt?   _No, wear a straight skirt._

2. Should I wear a long-sleeved shirt? _____

3. Should I wear casual clothes? _____

4. Should I wear a narrow tie? _____

5. Should I wear a heavy jacket? _____

6. Should I wear a short skirt? _____

7. Should I wear high heels? _____

8. Should I wear flared jeans? _____

Grammar Connection: **Present Progressive Tense** – *Who* **Questions**

| Who is wearing a skirt? | Laura is. |
| Who is wearing a skirt? | Laura and Amy are. |

Note:
- When *Who* is the subject of the sentence, it is singular.

C Answer these *Who* questions about the four people. Then, write two more questions and answers.

| Laura | Chad | Amy | Ryan |

1. Who is wearing a long-sleeved shirt? _____ *Chad is.* _____
2. Who is wearing low heels? _____
3. Who is wearing a polo shirt? _____
4. Who is wearing long pants? _____
5. Who _____ _____
6. Who _____ _____

CD 2
Track 4

D Listen to this young woman decide which clothes to wear. Match the clothes that she is going to wear.

Word Work Partners

Choose three pictures from a magazine. Describe the clothes that the people are wearing.

Fabrics and Patterns

A **Unscramble each word. What is the fabric?**

1. ertheal _____leather_____

2. loow _____

3. imden _____

4. oottcn _____

5. nonly _____

6. sherecam _____

7. nilne _____

8. ceal _____

9. tevlev _____

10. deeus _____

Grammar Connection: Comparative Adjectives

A velvet dress is **softer than** a lace dress.
A wool jacket is **heavier than** a nylon jacket.
A suede jacket is **more expensive than** a corduroy jacket.

Note:
- Comparative adjectives compare two people, places, or things.
- For one-syllable adjectives, add *er* + *than*.
- For two-syllable adjectives ending in *y*, change the *y* to *i* and add *er* + *than*.
- For other adjectives with two or more syllables, add *more than* before the adjective.

B **Complete each sentence with the comparative form of the adjective.**

1. A cashmere sweater is __*more expensive than*__ a wool sweater.   (expensive)

2. A silk robe is _____ a cotton robe.   (soft)

3. A silk tie is _____ a linen tie.   (fashionable)

4. A wool sweater is _____ a cotton sweater.   (warm)

5. Corduroy pants are _____ denim pants.   (heavy)

6. A lace dress is _____ a linen dress.   (formal)

7. A wool scarf is _____ a cotton scarf.   (warm)

8. A leather jacket is _____ a wool jacket.   (expensive)

9. A linen skirt is _____ a lace skirt. (comfortable)

C Write the pattern under each scarf.

1. _____solid_____ 2. _____ 3. _____ 4. _____

5. _____ 6. _____ 7. _____ 8. _____

CD 2
Track 5

D Listen to each conversation. Write the name of the pattern that the woman chooses under each picture.

Conversation 1:   Conversation 2:   Conversation 3:

_____   _____   _____

| Word Work | Partners |

Plan an outfit for each of these situations. Describe the clothing, the fabric, and the pattern.

1. Business meeting (man): _____*a navy wool suit with a polka dot silk tie*_____

2. Guest at a wedding (woman): _____

3. Teenage boy going to the movies on a cold day: _____

_____

4. Woman on a job interview: _____

Buying, Wearing, and Caring for Clothes

A **Circle the correct word.**

1. [(Zip up)   Sew on] your coat.

2. [Buckle   Button] your shirt.

3. [Hang up   Button up] your coat in the closet.

4. [Try on   Iron] the shoes.

5. [Cut off   Roll up] the price tag.

6. [Wash   Dry clean] the shirt in cold water.

7. [Press   Sew on] the button.

Grammar Connection: Simple Past Tense – Statements

> She **looked** for a jacket.
> She **bought** a wool jacket.
> She **wore** it to work.

Note:
- Regular past tense verbs end in *d* or *ed*.
- There are many irregular verbs in English. For example:

buy – bought	cut – cut	dry – dried	hang – hung
put – put	take – took	try – tried	wear – wore

B **Complete the story using these words.**

ironed	~~went shopping~~	hung	unbuttoned	put on
went into	sewed on	bought	tried on	took it home

Peter ___**went shopping**___ for a shirt to wear to a party. He saw three shirts that

he liked. He _____ the dressing room and _____

all three. He _____ the blue one and _____. When

he got home, he _____ the shirt to show his wife. One button was

loose. When he _____ the shirt, the button came off.

His wife _____ the button for him. Peter _____

the shirt and _____ it in his closet.

114

C **Write the correct response.**

Mend it.	Buy it.	Take it off.
Dry clean it.	~~Cut it off.~~	Roll them up.
Sew it on.	Iron it.	Wash it.

1. The price tag is still on my dress.   _Cut it off._

2. I'm too hot in this sweater.   _____

3. I spilled some coffee on my shirt.   _____

4. I have a rip in my sleeve.   _____

5. My button came off.   _____

6. I really like this dress.   _____

7. My shirt is wrinkled.   _____

8. The sleeves are too long.   _____

9. My leather jacket is dirty.   _____

CD 2
Track 6

D **Listen to each statement. Write the number of the statement under the correct picture.**

a. ____

b. ____

c. _1_

d. ____

e. ____

f. ____

g. ____

h. ____

Word Work **Partners**

Write three clothing items that you can wash. Write three clothing items that you have to dry clean.

Sewing and Laundry

A   **Complete the instructions for washing and drying clothes.**

1. Turn on the water in the washing machine. Add the ___laundry detergent___ and

   the _____. Put the clothes in the machine.

2. Take the _____ out of the washing machine. Put them in the

   _____.

3. When the clothes are dry, fold them. If some of the clothes are wrinkled, set up

   your _____ and heat up the _____.

Grammar Connection: Modals – *should / shouldn't*

> You **should wash** the sweater in cold water.
> You **shouldn't wash** the sweater in hot water.

Note:
- Use *should* and *shouldn't* to give advice or a suggestion.
- Use the base form of the verb after *should* and *shouldn't*.

B   **Read the care instructions. Complete the sentences with *should* or *shouldn't*.**

A

Machine wash
cold water
Tumble dry low
Do not iron

1. You ___should___ wash this item in cold water.

2. You _____ iron this item.

B

Machine wash cold
Delicate cycle
Line dry only

3. You _____ wash this item in hot water.

4. You _____ put this item in the dryer.

D

Machine wash with
dark colors warm water
Tumble dry low
Warm iron if needed

5. You _____ wash this item with dark colors.

6. You _____ use the low setting on the dryer.

C

Dry clean only

7. You _____ wash this item in a washing machine.

8. You _____ dry clean this item.

C Read each statement. Check *Possible* or *Not possible*.

		Possible	Not possible
1.	Take up a hem.	✓	___
2.	Put the pin in the pincushion.	___	___
3.	Measure the hem with a thimble.	___	___
4.	Put the thread through the needle.	___	___
5.	Sew on a sleeve with a safety pin.	___	___
6.	Iron the shirt with a hanger.	___	___
7.	Cut the thread with scissors.	___	___
8.	Sew on a pocket with a sewing machine.	___	___

CD 2
Track 7

D Listen and write the number of each statement under the correct shirt.

a. ___

b. ___

c. ___

d. ___

e. ___

f. _1_

Word Study

It's easy to draw pictures of many items, such as clothing. Choose six words that are difficult for you to remember. Copy the words and draw a picture next to each one to remind you of the word. Repeat the words, trying to remember the picture you drew for each one.

Vehicles and Traffic Signs

A **Complete the sentences.**

1. A ___tractor trailer___ transports items across the country.

2. The truck is pulling a _____ with horses in it.

3. You call a _____ if your car breaks down on the highway.

4. Many countries require a _____ rider to wear a helmet.

5. People in a _____ can ride with the top down in good weather.

6. A _____ carries dirt or sand to a construction site.

7. An _____ takes injured people to the hospital.

Grammar Connection: Simple Past Tense – Affirmative and Negative Statements

He **passed** the stop sign. He **drove** carefully.	He **didn't pass** the stop sign. He **didn't drive** carefully.

Note:
• Use *didn't* and the base form of the verb to form the negative in the past tense.

B **Fill in the correct form of the verb. Explain the reason that each person received a traffic ticket. Some answers are affirmative and some are negative.**

1. She (make) ___made___ an illegal U-turn.

2. She (stop) _____ at the stop sign.

3. He (go) _____ the wrong way on a one-way street.

4. She (drive) _____ carefully in a school zone.

5. He (pass) _____ a car in a no-passing zone.

6. She (yield) _____ when entering the highway.

7. He (stop) _____ for a pedestrian who was in a crosswalk.

8. She (make) _____ an illegal left-hand turn.

C **When you are driving, you must stop for certain vehicles when their lights are flashing. Write the names of four of these vehicles.**

1. ___a police car___   3. _____

2. _____   4. _____

D Complete the sentences with the names of vehicles. There are many correct answers.

1. _____A limousine_____ is more comfortable than _____a pickup truck_____.

2. _____ is faster than _____.

3. _____ is more expensive than _____.

4. _____ is better for a large family than _____.

5. _____ is more useful on a farm than _____.

CD 2
Track 8

E Listen to each statement. Write the number of the statement under the correct road sign.

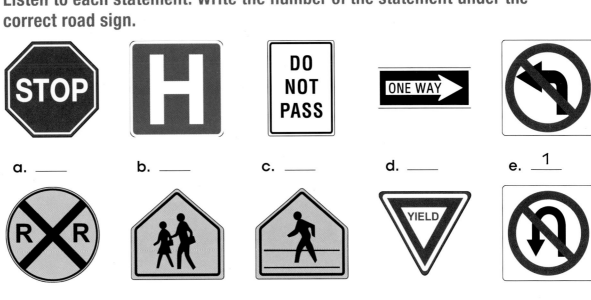

a. ____

b. ____

c. ____

d. ____

e. _1_

f. ____

g. ____

h. ____

i. ____

j. ____

Word Work Small Group

Guess the meaning of these road signs.

1.

2.

3.

4.

5.

6.

7.

8.

9.

10.

Parts of a Car

A Write the name of each part of this car.

1. _____
2. _____
3. _____
4. _____
5. _____
6. _____
7. _____
8. _____
9. _____
10. _____

Grammar Connection: *Because*

> I can't park the car on a hill **because the parking break doesn't work.**

Note:
- Use *because* to explain a reason.
- Put a subject and a verb after *because*.

B Complete the sentences with the correct part of a car.

1. I don't know how fast I'm going because the ____*speedometer*____ doesn't work.

2. I can't drive in the rain because the _____ don't work.

3. I can't listen to music because someone stole my _____.

4. I don't know if I need gas because the _____ doesn't work.

5. I can't see the road behind me because my _____ is missing.

6. I hope I don't get a flat tire because I don't have a _____.

7. I don't like to drive when it's cold because the _____ doesn't work.

C Complete each sentence with a word from Exercise A.

1. Put the key in the _____ignition_____.

2. Let's listen to some music. Turn on the _____.

3. Honk the _____.

4. Step on the _____. There is a stop sign ahead.

5. You're going too slowly. Step on the _____.

6. When you park on a hill, put on the _____.

7. It's hot in here. Turn on the _____.

8. Use the _____. Put the car in second gear.

9. Look in the _____. See if it's safe to pass.

10. Look at the _____. You're speeding!

CD 2
Track 9

D Listen as a father gives his daughter a driving listen. Listen to his first statement. Circle his next statement.

1. (a.) Step on the brake.   b. Step on the accelerator.

2. a. Put on the brake light.   b. Put on the turn signal.

3. a. Take off the gearshift.   b. Take off the emergency brake.

4. a. Honk the horn.   b. Turn off the ignition.

5. a. Check the rearview mirror.   b. Check the battery.

6. a. Turn on the radiator.   b. Turn on the headlights.

7. a. Turn on the windshield wipers.   b. Turn on the brake light.

Word Work Small Group

Take this driving quiz. Then, discuss your answers with your group.

1. You should pass another vehicle on the right.	True	False
2. Driving too slowly can cause an accident.	True	False
3. You can park in front of a fire hydrant.	True	False
4. When you enter a highway, you must yield to traffic.	True	False
5. Cars must stop for a pedestrian in a crosswalk.	True	False
6. You can talk on a hand-held cell phone when driving.	True	False

Road Trip

A Check the things you should do <u>before</u> you take a road trip.

_____	**1.** pack	_____	**5.** check the oil
_____	**2.** honk the horn	_____	**6.** put air in the tires
_____	**3.** get gas	_____	**7.** look at a map and check the directions
_____	**4.** get a speeding ticket	_____	**8.** pay a toll

Grammar Connection: **Past Time Clauses**

After they left their house,	they got on the highway.
When they got lost,	they looked at a map.

Note:
* Both the main clause and the time clause have a subject and a verb.
* In a past time clause sentence, both verbs are in the simple past tense.

B Match. What did this couple do on their road trip?

_f_ **1.** After they packed the car, **a.** they called 911.

_____ **2.** When they got gas, **b.** they asked for directions.

_____ **3.** When they got lost, **c.** they parked the car.

_____ **4.** When they passed a construction area, **d.** they checked the oil.

_____ **5.** When they saw an accident, **e.** they turned on the headlights.

_____ **6.** When they entered a tunnel, **f.** they left home.

_____ **7.** As they got off the highway, **g.** they paid the toll.

_____ **8.** When they arrived at the hotel, **h.** they slowed down.

C Number the sentences in the correct order.

_____ He gave me a speeding ticket.

_____ I pulled over to the side of the road.

_____ A police officer saw me and put on his flashing red lights.

_1_ I was speeding.

_____ I showed the officer my license and registration.

D Complete the story in the simple past tense.

Ben and Joji decided to go to the beach. They _____packed_____ their

towels, bathing suits, and a picnic lunch into the car. Before they

_____ the highway, they _____ gas and

_____ the oil. As they were driving, they heard a loud noise. They

_____ a flat tire. Ben _____ to the side of the road.

They _____ the tire and continued along the road. After an hour,

they _____ the toll and _____ the highway. They

_____ at the beach at 11:00. They _____ the car

and carried their things onto the beach.

CD 2
Track 10

E Listen to each statement and look at the picture. Circle *True* or *False*.

Picture 1	Picture 2	Picture 3
1. (True) False	1. True False	1. True False
2. True False	2. True False	2. True False
3. True False	3. True False	3. True False
4. True False	4. True False	4. True False

Word Work Small Group

Discuss or write the answers in your notebook. Explain
where you were and what you did in each situation.
1. Did you ever get lost?
2. Did you ever have a flat tire?
3. Did you ever get a ticket?
4. Did you ever have an accident?
5. Did you ever run out of gas?
6. Did you ever ask for directions?

Airport

A **Complete the sentences.**

1. A plane takes off and lands on a _____runway_____.

2. A _____ flies the plane.

3. Passengers must show a _____ at the ticket counter.

4. Passengers with electronic tickets can use the _____.

5. Passengers pass through a _____ at the security checkpoint.

6. A _____ is a small suitcase that a passenger takes onto the plane.

7. Passengers put their carry-on bags into the _____.

8. A _____ serves drinks and meals.

9. After the flight, passengers pick up their luggage in the _____.

10. Passengers from other countries must pass through _____.

Grammar Connection: Simple Past Tense – *Yes/No* Questions

Did	you he they	fly to Canada?	Yes, I did. Yes, he did. Yes, they did.	No, I didn't. No, he didn't. No, they didn't.

Note:
* In the simple past tense, begin a *Yes/No* question with *Did*.
* Use the base form of the verb after the subject.
* The form of *Yes/No* questions is the same for all persons.

B **Answer these questions about the picture.**

Steve

Carla

14A   14B   14C

EXIT

1. Did the plane leave on time? _____No, it didn't._____

2. Did Carla sit in an aisle seat? _____

3. Did she put her seat belt on? _____

4. Did Steve put his bag in the overhead compartment? _____

5. Did Carla and Steve sit in first class? _____

6. Did they go through security? _____

7. Did the plane take off yet? _____

C **Put the sentences in order.**

_____ Stand in line at the security checkpoint.

__1__ Check in and show your photo ID at the ticket counter.

_____ Walk to your gate.

_____ Go through the metal detector.

_____ Get your boarding pass.

_____ Show your boarding pass and photo ID to the security officer.

D **Read each statement. Circle _T_ for True or _F_ for False.**

1. You can buy your ticket at an automated check-in machine.   T   (F)

2. You must show your photo ID when you check in.   T   F

3. First class is more expensive than economy class.   T   F

4. You need to take off a metal belt at the security checkpoint.   T   F

5. You wait for your plane in the baggage claim area.   T   F

6. At customs, the official can check your bags.   T   F

CD 2
Track 11

E **Listen to each sentence. Where is each person? Write the number of the statement next to the correct area in the airport.**

_____ security checkpoint   _____ gate

__1__ customs   _____ baggage claim

_____ ticket counter   _____ immigration

Word Work **Small Group**

Discuss or write the answers in your notebook.

1. What is the nearest international airport to your house?

2. How often do you fly?

3. How long are the lines at the security checkpoint?

4. Do you buy airline tickets online or from a travel agent?

Taking a Flight

A In your notebook, write about each picture. What is happening?

1.

2.

3.

4.

5.

6.

Grammar Connection: Modals – *couldn't / had to*

We **couldn't use** our cell phones.
We **had to turn off** our cell phones.

Note:
- Use *could not* to show that something is not permitted or not possible.
- *Couldn't* is the contraction for *could not*. Use *couldn't* in conversation.
- Use *had to* show that something was necessary or required.
- Use the base form of the verb after *couldn't* and *had to*.

B Complete the sentences about an uncomfortable flight. Use *couldn't* or *had to*.

1. I _____*had to*_____ stand in line for one hour to go though security.

2. The plane _____ take off because of bad weather.

3. We _____ sit on the runway for four hours.

4. I _____ put my carry-on bag in the overhead compartments because they were full.

5. I _____ read my book because my light didn't work.

6. I _____ listen to music because the headphones were broken.

7. I _____ listen to a baby crying for three hours!

8. I _____ find my baggage. It went to the wrong airport.

C Read the two statements. If the meaning is the same, circle *S.* If the meaning is different, circle *D.*

1.	Check in.	Go to the ticket counter.	(S) D
2.	Go through security.	Walk through the metal detector.	S D
3.	Stow your bag.	Put your bag in the overhead compartment.	S D
4.	Board the plane.	Get off the plane.	S D
5.	Choose a meal.	Eat your meal.	S D
6.	Claim your bag.	Get your bag at the baggage claim area.	S D
7.	Fasten your seat belt.	Take off your seat belt.	S D

D Put the sentences in order.

____ Sit down and fasten your seat belt.

____ Take off.

_1_ Board the plane.

____ Stow your carry-on bag.

____ Find your seat.

CD 2
Track 12

E Look at the picture and listen to each statement. Write the seat number of the correct passenger.

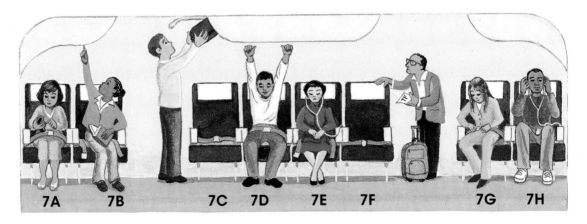

7A   7B   7C   7D   7E   7F   7G   7H

1. _7B_   3. ____   5. ____   7. ____

2. ____   4. ____   6. ____   8. ____

Word Work **Partners**

You are on a long international flight. Write three sentences in your notebook explaining how you will pass the time.

Example: **I will put my seat back, put on my headphones, and listen to music.**

Public Transportation

A **Complete the sentences.**

1. The _____subway_____ runs under the city.

2. If there are no seats, hold onto a pole or a _____.

3. A taxi can only carry three or four _____.

4. Each taxi has a _____ to show the fare.

5. A _____ can carry people and cars across a river.

6. You oan buy a train tickot at a _____.

7. Give your ticket to the _____ on the train.

8. A _____ gives information about the train times.

B **Read each statement. Check *Possible* or *Not Possible*.**

	Possible	Not Possible
1. Put a token in the turnstile.	✓	___
2. Wait on the platform for the train.	___	___
3. Give your ticket to the taxi driver.	___	___
4. Look at the meter for your fare.	___	___
5. Ride the subway under the city.	___	___

┌ **Grammar Connection: Comparative Adjectives Review** ┐

A subway is **faster than** a bus.
A subway is **noisier** than a bus.
A taxi is **more expensive than** a subway.

Note:
• Remember that comparative adjectives compare two people, places, or things.

C **Complete the sentences about different kinds of public transportation. There are many correct answers.**

1. A _____train_____ is more comfortable than _____a subway_____.

2. A _____ is quieter than _____.

3. A _____ is more expensive than _____.

4. A _____ is faster than _____.

5. A _____ is more crowded than _____.

6. A _____ is more convenient than _____.

D **Match the questions and answers.**

_d_ 1. Where can I get a taxi?　　　**a.** I take the bus.

___ 2. What's the fare?　　　**b.** On the platform.

___ 3. Where do I wait for the train?　　　**c.** I missed the bus.

___ 4. How do you get to work?　　　**d.** At the taxi stand.

___ 5. Where's your ticket?　　　**e.** It's $2.00.

___ 6. Why are you late?　　　**f.** I catch the 7:25.

___ 7. What train do you take?　　　**g.** I gave it to the conductor.

CD 2
Track 13

E **Listen to each statement. Circle the type of transportation each person is talking about — train, subway, or taxi.**

1.　**a.** train　　　**b.** subway　　　**(c.)** taxi

2.　**a.** train　　　**b.** subway　　　**c.** taxi

3.　**a.** train　　　**b.** subway　　　**c.** taxi

4.　**a.** train　　　**b.** subway　　　**c.** taxi

5.　**a.** train　　　**b.** subway　　　**c.** taxi

6.　**a.** train　　　**b.** subway　　　**c.** taxi

7.　**a.** train　　　**b.** subway　　　**c.** taxi

Word Work **Small Group**

Discuss or write the answers in your notebook.
1. When do you take public transportation?
2. Where do you wait?
3. How much is the fare?

Up, Over, Around

A **Circle the correct word.**

1. A bridge goes [(over) under] a river.

2. A subway travels [along   under] a city.

3. A plane flies [out of   over] an ocean.

4. I rode my bicycle [along   between] the river.

5. I swam [behind   across] the river.

6. We drove [through   between] the city.

7. I walked [over   toward] the town.

B **Write the opposite of each sentence.**

1. I drove into the tunnel.   *I drove out of the tunnel.*

2. I walked over the bridge.   _____

3. I took a left at the light.   _____

4. We made a right at the sign.   _____

5. They hiked up the mountain.   _____

6. Get onto Route 2 West.   _____

C **Write a direction line for each picture.**

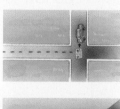

Turn left at the traffic light.

_____

_____

_____

_____

Grammar Connection: **Giving Directions**

	Note:
Go along the river. **Turn** right.	• When you give directions, use the base form of the verb.

D Look at the map. Write the directions from the house on Main Street to the library.

I am a librarian in the city and I drive to work. My house is on Main Street. I drive

_____**along**_____ Main Street and go _____ the Mill Bridge. After the

bridge, I get on Route 80 South. After I go _____ Blue Lake, I make a

_____ onto Route 10 East. I drive _____ the Midtown Tunnel and

_____ the city. I make a _____ onto 7th Avenue, and then a

_____ into the parking lot. The parking lot is _____ the library.

CD 2
Track 14

E Listen to the directions. In your notebook, take notes or draw a map. Compare your directions with a friend. Listen again and check the directions.

Word Work	Partners

Choose a well-known location in your city, such as the hospital or a museum. Write the directions from your school to that location.

Word Study

Talk to yourself in English. If you are alone, talk out loud. If you are in a store, on a bus, or in another location, "talk" in your head. Use your new vocabulary to describe what you see or what you are doing.

Example: *I'm driving south on Route 21. I'm going over a bridge. I'll get off at Exit 9. I need to stop for gas.*

The Human Body

A Complete the sentences.

1. You put a ring on your _____finger_____.

2. You put shoes on your _____.

3. You put a watch on your _____.

4. You put a hat on your _____.

5. You put a belt around your _____.

6. You put gloves on your _____.

B There are five senses. Write the part of the body you use for each one.

1. hearing: _____ears_____

2. seeing: _____

3. touching: _____

4. tasting: _____

5. smelling: _____

┌─ Grammar Connection: **Simple Present Tense – Third Person Statements**

| A muscle | **helps** | to move the body. |
| Muscles | **help** | to move the body. |

Note:
• For the simple present tense, add an *s* to the third person singular verb.

C Match the organ and its function. Then, circle the correct form of the verb.

_g_ 1. The liver   a. (help / helps) us to breath.

___ 2. The lungs   b. (digest / digests) food in the body.

___ 3. The brain   c. (help / helps) us to think and feel.

___ 4. The muscles   d. (pump / pumps) blood through the body.

___ 5. The stomach   e. (form / forms) the skeleton of the body.

___ 6. The bones   f. (clean / cleans) the blood.

___ 7. The skin   g. (process /(processes)) many substances in the body.

___ 8. The heart   h. (cover / covers) the body.

___ 9. The kidneys   i. (help / helps) us to move the body.

D **Listen to the directions for each of the three stretches. Complete the directions. Then, write the letter of each exercise under the correct picture.**

A. Lie on your ____back____ with your _____ bent. Slowly lift your

_____ and then your _____ off the floor. Hold for five seconds.

Slowly lower your _____ to the floor, starting with your _____.

B. Lie on your _____ with your _____ bent. Keep one _____

bent. Raise the other _____ to the ceiling. Hold the _____ with

both _____ and gently pull it toward your _____.

C. Lie on your _____ with your _____ bent. Raise and bend one

_____. Hold the _____ with both _____. With your

_____, make small circles in the air.

1. ____   2. ____   3. ____

Word Work **Partners**

Write four parts of your body you use to perform each action.

_____   _____   _____

_____   _____   _____

_____   _____   _____

_____   _____   _____

Illnesses, Injuries, Symptoms, and Disabilities

A **Look at the picture in your dictionary and complete the sentences.**

1. The woman in the green shirt has _____asthma_____.

2. Her little boy has an _____.

3. The girl in the pink shirt has _____ in her hair.

4. The boy in the white shirt has _____.

5. The woman in the blue jeans and print shirt has a _____.

6. The man in the gold shirt has a _____.

7. The man in the white shirt and dark glasses is _____.

8. The girl in the orange shirt is _____ and _____.

9. The delivery person is _____.

Grammar Connection: *How* Questions

| **How** did you sprain your ankle? | I slipped on the ice. |

Note:
- Use *How* to ask in what way or manner. In this question, *How* means "How did it happen?"

B **Write the correct answer next to each question.**

I ate too much.	I fell asleep on the beach.
I touched a hot pot.	~~I ate strawberries.~~
I caught it from my son.	My new shoes are too tight.

1. How did you get that rash?   _I ate strawberries._

2. How did you get that sunburn?   _____

3. How did you burn your hand?   _____

4. How did you get that blister?   _____

5. How did you get that cold?   _____

6. How did you get a stomachache?   _____

C Circle the correct word.

1. I caught a [(cold)   swollen ankle] from my friend.

2. I fell off my bike and I have a [sunburn   sprained wrist].

3. First, my daughter had [measles   a blister]. Then, my son caught it from her.

4. I drink tea when I have a [swollen ankle   sore throat].

5. Children can easily get [acne   lice] from one another.

6. My son has [mumps   asthma]. His face and neck are very swollen.

7. My mother has [measles   arthritis] in her hands and knees.

D Look at the Word Partnerships in your dictionary. Complete with *have* or *feel*.

1. I _____have_____ a sore throat.   4. I _____ a head cold.

2. I _____ dizzy.   5. I _____ nauseous.

3. I _____ a bad cold.   6. I _____ the flu.

E Listen to six people call in sick to work. Write the number of the conversation you hear next to the correct problem.

CD 2
Track 16

_____ **a.** dizzy   _____ **d.** a stomachache

_____ **b.** a bad cold   _1_ **e.** the flu

_____ **c.** chicken pox   _____ **f.** a sprained wrist

| Word Work | Small Group |

Ask each other about the illnesses and injuries in the chart. Talk or write about your experiences.

A: Did you ever have a bloody nose?
B: Yes. I was about nine years old. I had a fight with my brother, and he hit me!

	Name:	Name:	Name:
a bloody nose	_____	_____	_____
a bee sting	_____	_____	_____
a sprained wrist	_____	_____	_____
a rash	_____	_____	_____
the chicken pox	_____	_____	_____
the mumps	_____	_____	_____
the measles	_____	_____	_____

Hurting and Healing

A **Match the picture and the action.**

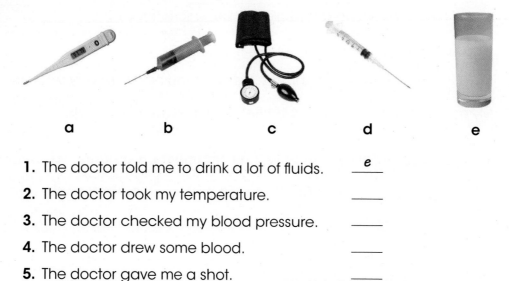

a   b   c   d   e

1. The doctor told me to drink a lot of fluids.   _e_
2. The doctor took my temperature.   ____
3. The doctor checked my blood pressure.   ____
4. The doctor drew some blood.   ____
5. The doctor gave me a shot.   ____

Grammar Connection: Past Time Clauses

| He had a heart attack | when he was running a marathon. |
| The child had an allergic reaction | when she ate some peanuts. |

Note:
- Both the main clause and the time clause have a subject and a verb.
- In a past time clause, both verbs are in the simple past tense.

B **Complete the sentences with the correct phrase. Put the verb in the past tense.**

| begin to choke | ~~break my arm~~ | get an electric shock |
| swallow poison | cut my foot | drown |

1. I ___broke my arm___ when I fell off my bicycle.
2. I _____ when I stepped on a piece of glass.
3. The man _____ when he fell out of a boat.
4. The man _____ when he was fixing a light.
5. The woman _____ when she was eating a piece of steak.
6. The child _____ when he found a bottle of bleach.

C Read the two statements. If the meaning is the same, write *S*. If the meaning is different, write *D*.

1. **a.** He took the pills.   **b.** He took the medication.   *S*

2. **a.** He overdosed on drugs.   **b.** He took too many pills.   ____

3. **a.** She burned her hand.   **b.** She cut her hand.   ____

4. **a.** She had a heart attack.   **b.** She went into shock.   ____

5. **a.** The doctor examined the man.   **b.** The doctor checked the man.   ____

6. **a.** He was in pain.   **b.** He was unconscious.   ____

7. **a.** She drank poison.   **b.** She swallowed poison.   ____

8. **a.** Drink fluids.   **b.** Drink liquids.   ____

CD 2
Track 17

D Listen to the conversation between a doctor and a patient. Read each statement and circle *T* for True or *F* for False.

1. The patient is sneezing and coughing.   (T)   F

2. The patient is vomiting.   T   F

3. The doctor examined the patient.   T   F

4. The doctor took her blood pressure.   T   F

5. The doctor took her temperature.   T   F

6. The doctor gave her a shot.   T   F

7. The patient should return to work tomorrow.   T   F

8. The patient should drink a lot of fluids.   T   F

9. The patient should take four pills a day.   T   F

Word Work **Partners**

This woman is at the doctor's office. She feels terrible. Write a short conversation between this patient and the doctor.

Hospital

A **Match.**

___f___ **1.** I need a nurse.

_____ **2.** Is my arm broken?

_____ **3.** I can walk.

_____ **4.** What's your blood type?

_____ **5.** Do you ever give blood?

_____ **6.** How bad was the cut?

_____ **7.** The patient needs more fluids.

a. No, you have to sit in the wheelchair.

b. It's B positive.

c. Start an IV.

d. Yes, I donate blood a few times a year.

e. We need to take an X-ray.

f. Press the call button.

g. I needed ten stitches.

Grammar Connection: Tense Contrast

Present Progressive Tense:	The nurse **is working** in the emergency room today.
Simple Present Tense:	The nurse **works** the evening shift.
Future Tense:	The nurse **is going to work** tomorrow.
Past Tense:	The nurse **worked** yesterday.

B **Complete the sentences about the hospital with the correct form of the verb.**

1. The paramedics (bring) _____are bringing_____ the patient into the emergency room now.

2. The man's wife (call) _____ 911 thirty minutes ago.

3. The patient (press) _____ the call button.

4. She (ask) _____ the nurse for a bedpan.

5. The surgeon (operate) _____ on the patient now.

6. The surgeon always (wear) _____ a mask when he operates.

7. The lab technician (take) _____ blood from the woman's arm.

8. The orderly (push) _____ the woman in a wheelchair.

9. She (cut) _____ her leg.

10. The doctor (put) _____ ten stitches in her leg.

C Write about each picture. What happened to each person? What is happening now? What is going to happen?

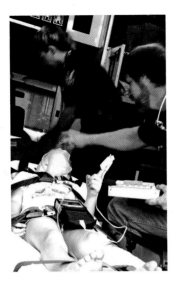  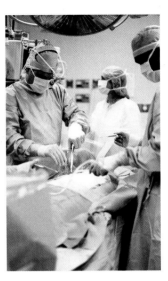

CD 2
Track 18

D Listen to the story about an emergency room patient. Circle *T* if the statement is true. Circle *F* if the statement is false.

1. Henry called for an ambulance.   T   (F)

2. Henry had a bad cut on his leg.   T   F

3. The paramedics started an IV.   T   F

4. The paramedics put Henry in a wheelchair.   T   F

5. Henry went to the intensive care unit.   T   F

6. The doctor ordered an X-ray of Henry's arm.   T   F

7. Henry needed an operation.   T   F

8. Henry needed thirty stitches in his arm.   T   F

Word Work **Small Group**

Look at the picture in the dictionary. Use your imagination to discuss or write the answers to these questions.

1. Why is the patient pressing the call button?

2. What happened to the man on the stretcher?

3. What did the lab technician just do?

4. Why does the patient in the emergency room need stitches?

5. What is the relationship between the visitor and the patient?

6. What kind of operation is the surgeon performing?

Medical Center

A Write the name of the specialist that each patient is visiting.

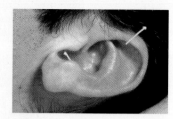

1. <u>orthopedist</u>   2. _____   3. _____

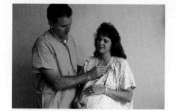

4. _____   5. _____   6. _____

Grammar Connection: Adjective Clauses with *who* and *that*

A pediatrician is a doctor **who treats children**.
An acupuncturist is a doctor **that treats diseases and pain with needles**.

Note:
- An adjective clause describes a noun.
- Use *who* or *that* to refer to people.

B Complete the sentences about each specialist. Use an adjective clause with *who* or *that*.

treat broken bones	examine eyes
treat the heart	care for the teeth
deal with pregnancy and childbirth	~~treat mental illness~~

1. A psychologist is a doctor <u>who treats mental illnesses</u>.

2. A dentist is a doctor _____.

3. A cardiologist is a doctor _____.

4. An optometrist is a doctor _____.

5. An orthopedist is a doctor _____.

6. An obstetrician is a doctor _____.

C **Complete the sentences with the correct procedure or equipment.**

filling	acupuncture	braces	contact lenses
~~EKG~~	crutches	cast	physical

1. You are having some chest pain. You need an _____EKG_____.

2. Your foot is broken. I need to put it in a _____.

3. You can't walk on that foot for six weeks. You need to use _____.

4. I know you don't like eyeglasses. You could try _____.

5. You have a cavity. You need a _____.

6. Your front teeth are not straight. You need _____.

7. You are a new patient. You will need a complete _____.

8. I always have this pain in my shoulder. I'm going to try _____.

CD 2
Track 19

D **Listen to each doctor. Write the number of each statement next to the correct specialist.**

_____ **a.** general practitioner   _____ **e.** optometrist

_____ **b.** dentist   _____ **f.** obstetrician

_____ **c.** cardiologist   _____ **g.** orthopedist

_____ **d.** acupuncturist   __1__ **h.** psychologist

Word Work **Small Group**

These are six other medical specialists. Discuss what they treat or do. Write a definition for each specialist.

podiatrist	dermatologist	plastic surgeon
neurologist	physical therapist	allergist

Example: **A podiatrist is a doctor who treats people's feet.**

Pharmacy

A Write the name of each item.

1. sterile tape

2. _____

3. _____

4. _____

5. _____

6. _____

7. _____

8. _____

Grammar Connection: *Why don't you ...?*

Why don't you	buy a cane? try a heating pad? use a humidifier?

Note:
- Use *Why don't you ...?* to give a suggestion.
- Use the base form of the verb after *Why don't you ...?*

B Give a suggestion for each illness or injury.

1. dry eyes: _____ Why don't you use some eyedrops? _____

2. a cut: _____

3. a cold: _____

4. a stomachache: _____

5. a sore throat: _____

6. a fever: _____

7. a headache: _____

8. allergies: _____

C Complete the words.

1. nasal ____spray____

2. hydrogen _____

3. prescription _____

4. warning _____

5. over-the-counter _____

6. knee _____

7. cough _____

8. ice _____

D Read each statement. Check *Good idea* or *Bad idea*.

	Good idea	Bad idea
2. Take cough syrup for a toothache.	____	✓
2. Use antibacterial ointment for a cut.	____	____
3. Use an ice pack for a sore throat.	____	____
4. Use a humidifier for a cold.	____	____
5. Use a nasal decongestant for a stomachache.	____	____
6. Use a heating pad for a sunburn.	____	____
7. Take lozenges for a backache.	____	____

CD 2
Track 20

E Paul sprained his ankle. Listen to the story. Then, listen to the questions and write the number of each question next to the correct answer.

____ a. He should take aspirin.

____ b. He should use a heating pad.

__1__ c. He should use an ice pack.

____ d. He should use a cane.

____ e. He should wear an elastic bandage.

Word Work Small Group

What do *you* do for each illness or injury?

1. When I have a cold, I _____.

2. When I have a fever, I _____.

3. When I have a sore throat, I _____.

Soap, Comb, and Floss

A Write the names of two products for each part of the body.

1. hair: _____shampoo_____ _____conditioner_____

2. teeth: _____ _____

3. skin: _____ _____

4. eyes: _____ _____

B Complete the names of these personal care products.

1. curling ____iron____   6. shaving _____

2. dental _____   7. _____ remover

3. face _____   8. _____ dryer

4. eye _____   9. electric _____

5. disposable _____   10. _____ clipper

Grammar Connection: Future Tense – *be going to*

I	am		
You We They	are	going to	use some deodorant.
He She	is		

Note:
• The future tense tells about things you plan to do tomorrow, next week, or some time in the future.

C What is each person going to use or do?

1. She just curled her hair. ___She's going to use some hair spray.___

2. Her hair is wet. _____

3. His hair is dirty. _____

4. She broke a fingernail. _____

5. They are going to the beach. _____

6. His hair is too long. _____

7. He just shaved. _____

8. You just sneezed. _____

D **Read each sentence. Check *Likely* or *Unlikely*.**

	Likely	Unlikely
1. She's washing her hair with sunscreen.	___	✓
2. She's putting blush on her nails.	___	___
3. He's shaving with an electric razor.	___	___
4. She's putting lipstick on her eyelashes.	___	___
5. He's putting deodorant on his hair.	___	___
6. She has a cold. She's using a tissue.	___	___
7. She's brushing her teeth with conditioner.	___	___

E **Listen to Eva's morning routine. Circle the personal care items that she uses.**

CD 2
Track 21

(toothbrush)	shampoo	curling iron	blush	nail polish
toothpaste	conditioner	lotion	eyeliner	brush
soap	blow dryer	face powder	deodorant	lipstick

Word Study

Use the notecard method.

• Write each word you want to learn on one side of a notecard.

• On the other side, draw a picture of the word or write the word in your language. Also, write a sentence on the card with the new word.

• Take out the cards once a day and study the new words.

• Add new words. Soon, you will have two piles of notecards: *Words I need to learn* and *Words I only need to review.*

razor	 He shaves his face with a razor every morning.

Jobs 1

A Complete the sentences with the name of the correct job.

1. _____A construction worker_____ can build a house.

2. _____ repairs and maintains computers.

3. _____ cleans offices and buildings.

4. _____ publishes books and magazines.

5. _____ plans roads, bridges, and tunnels.

6. _____ puts together products in a factory.

7. _____ sews shirts, dresses, and other clothing.

8. _____ designs logos and advertising for companies.

B Write six jobs that do not require a college education or a special license.

_____a delivery person_____   _____

_____   _____

_____   _____

Grammar Connection: Past Tense – *be*

I	**am**			I		
He She	**is**	a barber		He She	**was**	a barber.
You We They	**are**	a dentist		You We They	**were**	a dentist.

C Complete the sentences with the correct tense of the verb *be*.

1. I ____am____ a cashier. In my country, I ____was____ an accountant.

2. They _____ gardeners. In their country, they _____ farmers.

3. She _____ a hairstylist. In her country, she _____ a hairstylist, too.

4. He _____ a delivery person. In his country, he _____ a taxi driver.

5. She _____ a graphic artist. In her country, she _____ a college student.

6. We _____ carpenters. In our country, we _____ electricians.

7. I _____ a computer technician. In my country, I _____ an assembler.

8. We _____ cooks. In our country, we _____ cooks, too.

D Read each advertisement from the telephone book. Write the name of the job.

ART PARNESS, _____Accountant_____
• Income tax returns
• New business planning
• Personal financial planning
555-9872

KAPLIN BROTHERS, _____
• Indoor and outdoor lighting
• Air conditioning and ceiling fans
• Phone and cable wiring
555-3248

JOHN ELBAUM, _____
o Teeth whitening
o Crowns and bridges
o Full and partial dentures
555-6672

CARMEN GARCIA, _____
o Creative haircuts
o Permanents and straightening
o Custom coloring
555-4850

ANTON MICHAELS, _____
• Additions
• Custom home plans
• Complete planning and design
555-6549

JONG HO PARK, _____
• Creative designs for weddings
• Funeral arrangements
• Cut flowers from around the world
555-0945

E Listen to each speaker. Write the name of the correct job.

CD 2
Track 22

butcher	cashier	hairstylist	gardener
delivery person	~~architect~~	artist	babysitter

1. _____architect_____   5. _____

2. _____   6. _____

3. _____   7. _____

4. _____   8. _____

Word Work Small Group

Discuss the jobs in the dictionary. Complete the sentences.

1. _____ has a well-paid job.

2. _____ does the same thing over and over.

3. _____ is a blue-collar job.

4. _____ has good benefits.

5. _____ can run his/her own business.

Jobs 2

A Complete the sentences with the name of the correct job.

1. _____A pilot_____ flies a plane.

2. _____ plans vacations for clients.

3. _____ sells cars, furniture, or other items.

4. _____ takes pictures at weddings or other events.

5. _____ reports the news of important events.

6. _____ cares for sick or injured people

7. _____ drives a taxi.

8. _____ checks people who walk into a building.

9. _____ defends clients in court.

10. _____ buys and sells stocks and bonds.

Grammar Connection: Present Perfect Progressive Tense

I You They We	**have been**	**flying** a plane	for ten years.
He She	**has been**	**driving** a taxi	since 2010.

Note:
* The present perfect progressive tense talks about an action that started in the past and continues in the present time.

B Complete each sentence. Use the present perfect progressive tense.

1. He is a mechanic. He (fix) _____has been fixing_____ cars for three years.

2. She is a veterinarian. She (treat) _____ animals since 2000.

3. I am a salesperson. I (sell) _____ computers for one week.

4. They are nurses. They (care) _____ for patients for six years.

5. We are soldiers. We (protect) _____ our country for two years.

6. She is a locksmith. She (install) _____ locks since 2011.

7. I am a teacher. I (teach) _____ for ten years.

8. They are musicians. They (play) _____ in the orchestra since 2008.

C Write a good job for a person with each talent or interest.

1. A person who is good with numbers: *a stockbroker*

2. A person who loves animals: _____

3. A person who speaks well: _____

4. A person who enjoys performing for an audience: _____

5. A person who has good mechanical skills: _____

6. A person who enjoys traveling: _____

7. A person who likes children: _____

8. A person who is friendly and outgoing: _____

D Write eight jobs that a person can learn how to do on the job.

       a security guard _____   _____

_____   _____

_____   _____

_____   _____

CD 2
Track 23

E Listen to each statement. Who is each person speaking to?

1. _____ *a receptionist* _____   6. _____

2. _____   7. _____

3. _____   8. _____

4. _____   9. _____

5. _____   10. _____

Word Work Small Group

Discuss or write the answer to each question in your notebook.

1. If you were a musician, what instrument would you like to play?

2. If you were a pilot, what country would you like to fly to?

3. If you were a taxi driver, what city would you like to drive in?

4. If you were a receptionist, what kind of office would you like to work in?

5. If you were a salesperson, what product would you like to sell?

6. If you were a high school teacher, what subject would you like to teach?

Working

A **In your notebook, write about each person. What does each person do?**

1.

2.

3.

4.

5.

6.

7.

8.

1. _____ This person designs houses. _____

Grammar Connection: **Present Perfect Progressive Tense – *for* and *since***

For	Since
for a few minutes	**since** 9:00
for an hour	**since** 2010
for two weeks	**since** Monday
for three years	**since** she arrived

Note:
- Use *for* to show an amount of time.
- Use *since* to tell when an action started.

B **Complete the sentences with *for* or *since*.**

1. She has been singing ____*since*____ 10:00.

2. They have been loading the truck _____ two hours.

3. He has been cooking _____ 5:00.

4. He has been speaking _____ an hour.

5. They have been selling cars _____ 2000.

6. She has been delivering pizzas _____ two hours.

7. He have been making copies _____ for a half hour.

8. I have been typing _____ I got into the office.

9. He has been managing the company _____ five years.

10. They have been performing in the show _____ March.

C **Check the duties of an office assistant.**

_____ **1.** To take messages

_____ **2.** To cook lunch for the boss

_____ **3.** To open the mail

_____ **4.** To type letters and reports

_____ **5.** To make company decisions

_____ **6.** To call in sick

_____ **7.** To make copies

_____ **8.** To staple reports

_____ **9.** To hire new salespeople

_____ **10.** To use the computer

_____ **11.** To manufacture office supplies

_____ **12.** To file papers and reports

D **Listen to each person. What is the person doing?**

CD 2
Track 24

1. _She's using a computer._ _____

2. _____

3. _____

4. _____

5. _____

6. _____

7. _____

Word Work **Partners**

Read each sentence. Then, write another example for each verb.

1. File a letter. _File a report._

2. Design a kitchen. _Design a_

3. Manage a company. _____

4. Repair a bicycle. _____

5. Manufacture cameras. _____

6. Open the mail. _____

7. Plan a wedding. _____

8. Hire a painter. _____

Farm

A Write the name of the baby animal.

1. <u>   a kid   </u>   2. _____   3. _____

4. _____   5. _____   6. _____

B Put the steps in order.

_____ **a.** Water the seeds.   <u>1</u> **d.** Plow the field with the tractor.

_____ **b.** Plant corn seeds in the soil.   _____ **e.** Pick the corn.

_____ **c.** Put the corn in the silo.   _____ **f.** Watch the corn grow.

┌─ **Grammar Connection: *What is it called?*** ─┐

A baby cat **is called** a kitten.
A baby sheep **is called** a lamb.

C What is each baby animal called? Complete the sentences.

1. A baby dog <u>is called a puppy.</u>

2. A baby cow _____

3. A baby pig _____

4. A baby chicken _____

5. A baby goat _____

6. A baby rabbit _____

D **Complete the paragraph.**

Mr. and Mrs. Jones are farmers. They live in a _____farmhouse_____. There is a

lot of work on the farm. Mr. Jones has four _____ to help him.

Mr. Jones gets up at 5:00 in the morning. He _____ the cows and

_____ the pigs and the horses. Mrs. Jones gets up early, too.

She gathers the eggs from the _____. Mr. Jones grows several

kinds of _____—corn, wheat, and alfalfa. He plows the

_____ in the spring with his _____. There is a

_____ in the field to keep the birds away. Every day, he checks

the apple trees in the _____ and the grapes in the

_____. In the fall, he _____ the apples from

the trees.

CD 2
Track 25

E **Look at each picture and listen to the statement. Circle *T* if the statement is true. Circle *F* if the statement is false.**

1. T F	**4.** T F	**7.** T F	**10.** T F
2. T F	**5.** T F	**8.** T F	**11.** T F
3. T F	**6.** T F	**9.** T F	**12.** T F

Word Work **Partners**

Did you ever visit or live on a farm? List five things that you
did or that you saw.

Examples: **I gathered the eggs. I rode on the tractor.**

Office

A Write the names of eight office items or people you see in the picture.

thumbtacks

_____   _____

_____   _____

_____   _____

_____   _____

Grammar Connection: **Offers to Help with *I'll***

I'll fix it the printer. **I'll file** the reports.	Note: • We can use *I'll* to offer to help someone. • Use the base form of the verb after *I'll*.

B Write the office manager's response to each request from the boss. Begin each sentence with *I'll*.

put them in the shredder	send it on the fax machine
~~look in the file cabinet~~	get them from the supply cabinet
make them on the copy machine	get you her resume

1. Where are the old sales reports? __I'll look in the file cabinet.__

2. I need three copies of this report. _____

3. We need some more pencils. _____

4. I'm interviewing Ms. Sims in five minutes. _____

5. The lawyer needs this letter immediately. _____

6. We don't need these reports anymore. _____

c Look at the office in your dictionary. Write the location of each item.

1. Where is the business card file? _____It's on the right side of the desk._____

2. Where are the binders? _____

3. Where is the tape? _____

4. Where is the shredder? _____

5. Where is the resume? _____

6. Where is the pencil sharpener? _____

7. Where is the photocopy? _____

8. Where is the large file folder? _____

9. Where is the fax machine? _____

10. Where is the office manager? _____

CD 2
Track 26

D Listen to each request. Write the number of the request next to the correct item or equipment.

_____ **a.** letterhead   _____ **e.** file cabinet

_____ **b.** calculator   _____ **f.** telephone

_____ **c.** pencil sharpener   _____ **g.** correction fluid

__1__ **d.** sticky note   _____ **h.** thumbtack

Word Work Partners

How is a company office today different from an office 100 years ago?
Write six office items that were not used in offices 100 years ago.

_____   _____

_____   _____

_____   _____

Factory

A Look at the picture of the factory in the dictionary. Circle *T* if the statement is true. Circle *F* if the statement is false.

1. There are four workers on the assembly line.   (T)   F
2. All the workers on the assembly line are wearing hairnets.   T   F
3. The machine operator is wearing safety earmuffs.   T   F
4. There are eight boxes on the forklift.   T   F
5. There's a truck at the loading dock.   T   F
6. A worker is loading boxes on the truck with a dolly.   T   F
7. The shipping clerk is wearing a hard hat.   T   F

Grammar Connection: Modals – *have to / doesn't have to*

Packers **have to** wear safety boots. A packer **has to** wear safety boots.	Packers **don't have to** wear safety vests. A packer **doesn't have to** wear a safety vest.

Note:
* *Have to / has to* show that an action is necessary.
* *Don't have to / doesn't have to* show that an action is not necessary.
* Use the base form of the verb after modals.

B Look at the picture of the factory in your dictionary. Complete the sentences with *have to, has to, don't have to*, or *doesn't have to*.

1. The workers _____ *have to* _____ wear safety equipment.
2. Each worker _____ punch a time card.
3. The supervisor _____ wear a hair net.
4. The workers _____ follow safety regulations.
5. The machine operator _____ wear a safety visor.
6. The workers _____ wear respirators.
7. The forklift operator _____ drive slowly.
8. Robots _____ take beaks.
9. The factory _____ have a fire extinguisher.
10. The secretary _____ wear a hard hat.

c **Match each hazard with an example.**

___d___ **1.** biohazard   **a.** wires and cables

_____ **2.** electrical hazard   **b.** gasoline

_____ **3.** explosive materials   **c.** arsenic

_____ **4.** flammable materials   **d.** medical waste

_____ **5.** poisonous materials   **e.** uranium

_____ **6.** radioactive materials   **f.** dynamite

CD 2
Track 27

D **Listen to each sentence and circle the letter(s) of the correct worker. If none of the workers is wearing the equipment, circle *None*.**

       A   B   C   D

1. A   B   C   D   (None)   **6.** A   B   C   D   None

2. A   B   C   D   None   **7.** A   B   C   D   None

3. A   B   C   D   None   **8.** A   B   C   D   None

4. A   B   C   D   None   **9.** A   B   C   D   None

5. A   B   C   D   None   **10.** A   B   C   D   None

Word Work   **Small Group**

Write three rules for the factory in your dictionary.

Examples:

All workers have to punch their time cards as soon as they report to work.

All workers have to call the front office if they are going to miss a day of work.

Hotel

A **Complete the sentences.**

1. We have _____single rooms_____,

   _____, and large

   _____suites_____.

2. You can attend a meeting in one of our _____.

3. You can use the computers or make copies in our _____.

4. You can ask the _____ to get you tickets for a show.

5. You can buy souvenirs in our _____.

6. You can sit and relax in our _____.

7. You can celebrate a wedding or have a party in our _____.

8. You can exercise in our _____.

9. You can order dinner from our four-star _____.

Grammar Connection: Past Tense – *be*

The desk clerk	**was** **wasn't**	friendly. helpful.
The desk clerks	**were** **weren't**	

B *Use was, wasn't, were,* or *weren't* to complete the sentences about an uncomfortable hotel stay.

1. The room _____wasn't_____ clean.

2. The Internet in the business center _____ working.

3. The gift shop _____ closed.

4. The concierge _____ helpful.

5. The beds _____ comfortable.

6. The towels _____ dirty.

7. The escalator _____ broken.

8. Room service _____ very slow.

9. The guests in the next room _____ very noisy.

10. The room rates _____ very high!

C **Write the correct response.**

You can order from room service.	You can use the business center.
Call valet parking.	I'll call the bellhop.
In the ballroom.	You can ask the concierge.
~~I'll call a housekeeper.~~	It's 11:00 a.m.

1. Our bed hasn't been made. _____*I'll call a housekeeper.*_____

2. We have four suitcases. _____

3. I need to send a fax. _____

4. We would like dinner in our room. _____

5. Where is the art museum? _____

6. What time is check-out? _____

7. We need the car at 7:00 p.m. _____

8. Where is the wedding reception? _____

CD 2
Track 28

D **Listen to the conversation between a desk clerk and a caller. Complete the information.**

1. The caller made a reservation for _____ nights.

2. She wants a [single room   double room   suite].

3. The room rate is _____ a night.

4. Check-in time is _____. Check-out time is _____.

5. The caller asked about the following features [fitness center   sauna   business center   ballroom   gift shop   pool].

6. Parking is [free   an additional charge].

Word Work | **Partners**

You are going to spend the weekend at a hotel. What are the six most important features you consider?

_____   _____   _____

_____   _____   _____

Tools and Supplies 1

A What tool is each person using?

1. <u>a hammer</u> 2. _____ 3. _____ 4. _____

5. _____ 6. _____ 7. _____ 8. _____

Grammar Connection: Showing Purpose with *to*

> Use a ruler **to measure wood**.
> Use a utility wrench **to turn a bolt**.

Note:
- Use *to* + verb to show purpose.
- Use the base form of the verb after *to*.

B Match the tool and its purpose for the workers in Exercise A.

<u> c </u> 1. Use a hammer   **a.** to chop down a tree.

_____ 2. Use a drill   **b.** to make wood smooth.

_____ 3. Use a pipe wrench   **c.** to put a nail in the wall.

_____ 4. Use a power sander   **d.** to tighter a pipe.

_____ 5. Use a circular saw   **e.** to dig a hole.

_____ 6. Use a router   **f.** to make a small hole in a wall.

_____ 7. Use a shovel   **g.** to cut a piece of wood.

_____ 8. Use an ax   **h.** to make a decorative edge.

C Complete the questions.

1. Dig a hole.   Where's the _____?

2. Sand the wood.   Where's the _____?

3. Drill a hole.   Where's the _____?

4. Caulk the shower.   Where's the _____?

5. Break the rock.   Where's the _____?

6. Hold the wood tightly. Where's the _____?

7. Turn the screw.   Where's the _____?

CD 2
Track 29

D Listen and write the price under the correct item in the hardware store advertisement.

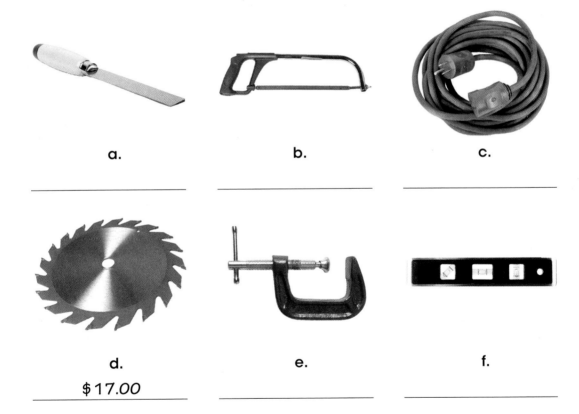

a.

b.

c.

_____

_____

_____

d.

e.

f.

$17.00

_____

_____

| Word Work | Partners |

You are going to buy tools for a small toolbox. Which six tools will you buy first?

_____   _____   _____

_____   _____   _____

Tools and Supplies 2

A **Complete the sentences.**

1. You put _____insulation_____ in the wall to keep a house warm.

2. You hammer a _____ into a wall.

3. You use a wrench to turn a _____.

4. You put _____ in a flashlight.

5. You turn a _____ with a screwdriver

6. You build the frame of a house with _____.

7. You put _____ on a bathroom floor.

8. You hang a door on _____.

| hinges |
| batteries |
| screw |
| ~~insulation~~ |
| board lumber |
| tile |
| nut |
| nail |

Grammar Connection: Modals – *should / shouldn't*

| You | **should** | hang the picture with a nail. |
| | **shouldn't** | hang the pictures with a screw. |

Note:
- Use *should* and *shouldn't* to give suggestions and opinions.
- Use the base form of the verb after *should* and *shouldn't*.

B **Complete the statements with *should* or *shouldn't*.**

1. You _____shouldn't_____ hang a mirror with duct tape.

2. You _____ paint a window with a paint roller.

3. You _____ measure carefully before you cut wood.

4. You _____ use an anchor when you hang a heavy picture.

5. You _____ put old batteries in a flashlight.

6. You _____ put insulation in the walls.

7. You _____ sandpaper the wall before you paint it.

8. You _____ install a hinge with nails.

C These workers are putting up drywall in a room. Write the tools and supplies that the workers need for each step.

1. Insulate the wall: _____insulation_____

2. Measure and cut the drywall: _____

3. Put up the drywall: _____

4. Tape and spackle the seams: _____

5. Sand the seams: _____

6. Paint the walls: _____

D Listen to this order for a hardware store. Complete the list of items.

CD 2
Track 30

Quantity/Item

6 sheets of _____   2 rolls of _____

4 sheets of _____   4 door _____

2 boxes of _____   3 packages of _____

3 boxes of _____

Word Work Small Group

Pretend you are going to build a bookcase. What tools and supplies do you need? Write out the steps you need to follow.

Drill, Sand, Paint

In your notebook, write a sentence about each picture. What is each worker doing?

1.

2.

3.

4.

CD 2
Track 31

B **Listen to the conversation between two friends. Answer the questions.**

1. Did the workers pour the concrete?   (Yes)   No

2. Did they dig a trench around the house?   Yes   No

3. Did they install the windows?   Yes   No

4. Did they put up the drywall?   Yes   No

5. Did they wire the house?   Yes   No

6. Did they cut and install the pipes?   Yes   No

7. Did they paint the house?   Yes   No

Grammar Connection: Simple Past Tense – Statements

She **installed** a cabinet.
He **tore down** a wall.

Note:
- Regular past tense verbs end in *d* or *ed*.
- There are many irregular verbs in English. For example:

  cut – cut   dig – dug   lay – laid   put – put   read – read   tear – tore

C **Complete the sentences with the correct past tense verb.**

1. He _____tore down_____ the wall with a sledgehammer.
2. He _____ the wood with a saw.
3. She _____ the room with a roller.
4. He _____ the house for electricity.
5. I _____ a trench with a shovel.
6. She _____ the wood with a tape measure.
7. He _____ a hole with a drill.
8. He _____ a ladder to get to the roof.
9. He _____ a new light in the kitchen.
10. She _____ the wood to make it smooth.

measure
wire
drill
plane
climb
cut
install
~~tear down~~
paint
dig

Word Work **Small Group**

Discuss or write the answers to the questions about building a house.
1. Which jobs require the most experience?
2. Which jobs require power tools?
3. Which jobs require a worker to measure carefully?

Word Study

Analyze your vocabulary study. For one week, record your study time and your study activities. How much time do you study vocabulary? What activities or methods are most effective for you? At the end of the week, have a class discussion. Different students can explain the activities that are helpful for them.

Example:

Day	Time	Activities
Monday	10 minutes	Vocabulary notecards
Tuesday	15 minutes	I studied the words on pages 158 and 159. I highlighted the words that were new for me and said them aloud.
Wednesday	15 minutes	Vocabulary notecards I wrote two new words in my vocabulary journal and wrote sentences with them.
Monday	_____	_____
Tuesday	_____	_____
Wednesday	_____	_____
Thursday	_____	_____
Friday	_____	_____
Saturday	_____	_____

Weather

A **Complete the sentences.**

1. A strong _____ wind _____ blew the tree down.

2. Sometimes there is a _____ in the sky after a rainstorm.

3. School was closed for a week because we had three feet of _____.

4. The lake is frozen. The _____ is ten inches thick.

5. It's raining lightly. I can see _____ on the window.

6. Look at those gray _____. It's going to rain.

7. The _____ shows that it is 30° outside.

8. It isn't going to snow because the temperature is above _____.

Grammar Connection: Noun and Adjective Forms with _y_

Noun	Adjective
rain	rainy
storm	stormy

Note:
- Many nouns have an adjective form.
- One common adjective ending is _y_.

B **Write the missing word form. Then, complete the sentences with the correct form of the word.**

Noun	Adjective	
1. sun	_____ sunny _____	It's _____ today.
2. _____	rainy	People use umbrellas on _____ days.
3. _____	stormy	We're going to have a bad _____.
4. wind	_____	It was so _____ that my hat blew off.
5. _____	cloudy	There isn't a _____ in the sky.
6. _____	foggy	It's difficult to drive in this _____.
7. _____	snowy	The _____ is very deep.
8. _____	icy	Don't slip on the _____.

C In your notebook, write about the weather conditions in these photos. What do you think the temperature is? What are the people doing?

CD 3
Track 1

D Listen to the international weather report. Write the temperature and forecast for today and tomorrow for each country.

Country	Weather Today	Weather Tomorrow
Poland	very cold	heavy snow
Australia		
Japan		
Mexico		
Colombia		
France		

Word Work Partners

Some countries have four seasons. Other countries have two seasons. How many seasons do you have in your country? Describe the weather in each season. What is the average temperature for each season?

The Earth's Surface

A Write the word for each feature of the Earth's surface.

1. <u>stream</u>   2. _____   3. _____   4. _____

5. _____   6. _____   7. _____   8. _____

Grammar Connection: Articles – a, an, the

> **A** beach is a sandy area near a lake or ocean.
> **The** beach was crowded yesterday.

Note:
- Use *a* or *an* to talk about a place or thing in general.
- Use *the* to talk about a specific place or thing.

B Complete the sentences with *a*, *an*, or *the*.

1. <u>An</u> island is a piece of land surrounded by water.

2. I took a photograph of _____ waterfall.

3. _____ desert is usually hot in the daytime and cold at night.

4. Before _____ volcano erupted, the people evacuated from the city.

5. _____ sandy beach is more comfortable than _____ rocky beach.

6. _____ glaciers in Alaska are a popular tourist attraction.

7. _____ ocean is a large body of salt water.

8. In the winter, _____ mountains near my house receive a lot of snow.

9. _____ peak is the highest part of a mountain.

C Write the names of nine features you see on this map.

peninsula	_____	_____
_____	_____	_____
_____	_____	_____

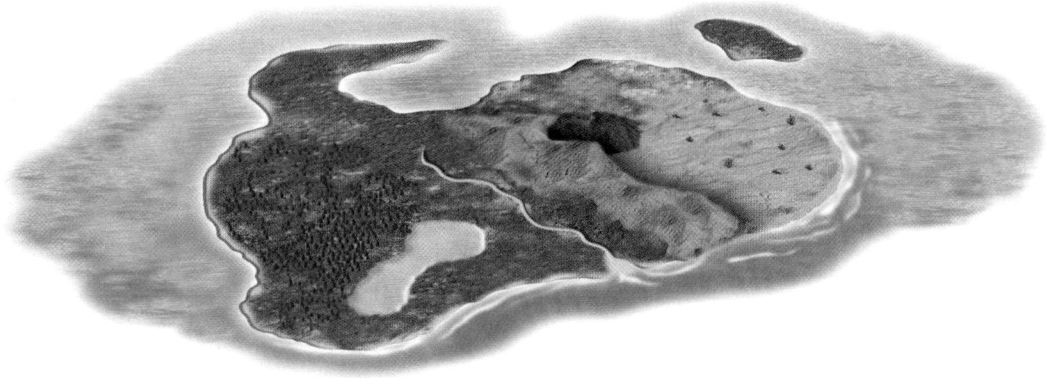

D Read the names of the places. Then, write the name of the feature.

Places	Feature
1. Sahara, Gobi, Patagonia	desert
2. Everest, K2, Denali	_____
3. Greenland, Borneo, Hawaii	_____
4. Andes, Himalayas, Rockies	_____
5. Amazon, Nile, Yangtze	_____
6. Pacific, Atlantic, Indian	_____

CD 3
Track 2

E Listen to the story of a long drive across the country. Write the nine features that are included in the story.

1. mountain range   4. _____   7. _____

2. _____   5. _____   8. _____

3. _____   6. _____   9. _____

Word Work Small Group

What country do you live in?

Draw a map of the country or state you live in. Show the major geographic features, such as mountain ranges, lakes, rivers, deserts, and islands.

Energy, Pollution, and Natural Disasters

A Write the name of the type of energy in each picture.

1. hydroelectric power

2. _____

3. _____

4. _____

5. _____

6. _____

Grammar Connection: Modals – *couldn't* / *had to*

We	**had to evacuate**	our home.
We	**couldn't stay**	in our home.

Note:
- *Had to* shows necessity or obligation.
- *Couldn't* shows that an action was not possible.

B Complete the sentences with the correct modal: *had to* or *couldn't*.

1. The avalanche covered the road. The police ____had to____ close the highway.

2. Everyone _____ evacuate their homes during the forest fires.

   We _____ stay with friends and relatives.

3. Many people lost their homes in the forest fire. They _____ file insurance claims for the damage.

4. After the flood, people _____ travel by boat.

5. The children _____ go to school for three days after the blizzard.

6. After the blizzard, we _____ shovel our driveway.

7. We lost power after the earthquake. We _____ use our computers.

8. Before the hurricane, we _____ buy extra food and batteries.

C Read the descriptions of the natural disasters and complete the sentences.

1. Many people died during the ____famine____ because there wasn't enough food.

2. We had a bad _____ last winter. It snowed for three days. All the schools and businesses in our city closed.

3. There was a minor _____ in the city. The buildings shook, but none of them collapsed.

4. A large _____ hit the coast, killing all the people on the beach.

5. The heavy rain caused a _____. People could only travel by boat.

6. During the _____, people watched fire and smoke shoot out of the mountain. Hot lava flowed down the sides of the mountain.

D Listen to the three conversations. Write the number of the conversation under the correct picture.

CD 3
Track 3

a. _____   b. _____   c. _____

E Write the names of five disasters that give people no warning. Write the names of five disasters that people know about a few hours or days before.

Disasters with no warning	Disasters with warning time
tornado	blizzard

Word Work Small Group

Talk or write about a disaster that occurred in your country.
What happened?

The United States and Canada

A Write the name of the correct state or capital.

1. _____California_____ is the largest state on the West Coast.

2. _____ is the largest state in the Southwest. The capital is

   _____ .

3. _____ in on both the Atlantic Ocean and the Gulf of Mexico.

4. _____ is a group of islands in the Pacific Ocean.

5. _____ is the largest state in the United States. It borders both

   British Columbia and the Yukon. The capital is _____ .

6. _____ is the capital of Canada.

Grammar Connection: Superlative Adjectives

Rhode Island is **the smallest** state.
Hawaii is **the rainiest** state.
New Jersey is **the most crowded** state.

Note:
- Superlative adjectives compare three or more people, places, or things.
- For one-syllable adjectives, add *the* + *est*.
- For two-syllable adjectives ending in *y*, change the *y* to *i* and add *the* + *est*.
- For other adjectives with two or more syllables, add *the most* before the adjective.

B Complete each sentence with the superlative form of the adjective.

1. Alaska is (large) _____the largest_____ state.

2. Arizona is (sunny) _____ state.

3. California is (populated) _____ state.

4. Nevada is (dry) _____ state.

5. Florida is (hot) _____ state.

6. Hawai'i is (expensive) _____ state to live in.

7. Alaska is (snowy) _____ state.

8. Louisiana is (wet) _____ state.

c Write the names of the states or provinces you will drive through to reach each destination.

1. From Washington, D.C., to Florida: ___Virginia___, _____

   , _____, _____

2. From Sacramento, California, to Springfield, Illinois: ___Nevada___,

   _____, _____, _____

3. From Phoenix, Arizona, to Nashville, Tennessee: _____,

   _____, _____, _____

   _____

4. From Quebec City, Quebec, to Victoria, British Columbia: _____

   , _____, _____, _____

CD 3
Track 4

D Listen to the information about the national parks. Write the name of the state where you find each park.

1. ___Colorado___   2. _____   3. _____

4. _____   5. _____   6. _____

| Word Work | Small Group |

Draw a state or a province. Add the bordering states, provinces, or territories one at a time. Who in the group can name the state or province first?

The World

A **Read each fact. Write the name of a continent or a country.**

1. _____ Asia _____ is the largest continent.

2. _____ is a continent with no permanent residents.

3. _____ is a continent with only one country.

4. _____ is a large country in both Asia and Europe.

5. _____ is the largest country in South America in size.

6. _____ is a country in Europe with no seaport.

7. _____ is an island country in Asia.

8. _____ is a country on both the Atlantic and Pacific oceans.

9. _____ is the southernmost country in Africa.

Grammar Connection: *Wh–* Questions with *be*

What is the capital of Brazil?
What is the official language of Brazil?

B **Write a question for the underlined answer.**

1. _____ What is the capital of Brazil? _____

   The capital of Brazil is <u>Brasília</u>.

2. _____

   The official language of Brazil is <u>Portuguese</u>.

3. _____

   The population of Brazil is <u>200 million</u>.

4. _____

   The currency of Brazil is <u>the real</u>.

5. _____

   The largest city in Brazil is <u>São Paulo</u>.

6. _____

   The most popular sport in Brazil is <u>football</u>.

CD 3
Track 5

C The world population is more than seven billion people. The pie chart shows the percentage of the world's population that lives on each continent. Listen and write the name of the correct continent on each part of the chart.

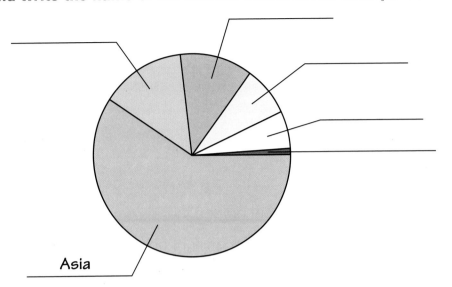

Asia

CD 3
Track 5

D Listen again. Write the population of each continent.

Asia _____   South America _____

Africa _____   Australia _____

Europe _____   Antarctica _____

North America _____

Word Work	Small Group

India	Japan	Russia	Brazil	Indonesia	Philippines
~~China~~	Turkey	Pakistan	Nigeria	South Korea	Bangladesh

These are twelve of the largest cities in the world in terms of population. Write the country for each city.

1. Shanghai, _____China_____   7. Manila, _____

2. Karachi, _____   8. São Paulo, _____

3. Mumbai, _____   9. Seoul, _____

4. Dhaka, _____   10. Jakarta, _____

5. Moscow, _____   11. Tokyo, _____

6. Istanbul, _____   12. Lagos, _____

The Universe

A **Write the correct word.**

| star | orbit | astronomers | space station | atmosphere |
| telescopes | satellites | planets | rocket | ~~sun~~ |

1. The largest body in our solar system is the _____sun_____.

2. The _____ are very large, ball-shaped bodies that move around the sun. The movement around the sun is called an _____.

3. A _____ is a bright ball of hot gas in the sky.

4. The _____ is the air above Earth.

5. _____ work in an observatory. They look at the solar system through _____.

6. A _____ is a spacecraft in which astronauts can live and work for long periods of time. A _____ takes astronauts into space.

7. Weather _____ send pictures and weather data from space.

Grammar Connection: Predictions with *will*

> Someday, people **will visit** Mars on vacation.
> Computer tablets **will replace** books in schools.

Note:
* Use *will* to make predictions about the future.
* Use the base form of the verb after *will*.

B **Complete these predictions. Then, write one more prediction about the future.**

1. Solar and wind power (provide) _____will provide_____ all energy on Earth.

2. People (plan) _____ vacations to space station hotels.

3. A large meteor (pass) _____ very close to Earth.

4. The Arctic (be) _____ ice-free in the summer.

5. People (live) _____ to the age of 120.

6. Scientists (discover) _____ life on a distant planet.

7. _____

C Unscramble the planets.

1. snurua   Uranus   _____

2. snuve   _____

3. repitjut   _____

4. harte   _____

5. sram   _____

6. petnnue   _____

7. runtas   _____

8. cryurem   _____

CD 3
Track 6

D Listen to the information about the universe. Then, circle *T* if the statement is true or *F* if the statement is false.

1. The sun is a planet.   T   (F)

2. The sun is made of gases.   T   F

3. Earth is the center of the universe.   T   F

4. All planets travel in the same orbit.   T   F

5. Earth is the first planet from the sun.   T   F

6. It takes 365 days for Earth to orbit the sun.   T   F

7. Every 24 hours Earth turns on its axis.   T   F

8. The area facing the sun has night.   T   F

9. The moon orbits Earth.   T   F

10. It takes one year for the moon to orbit Earth.   T   F

Word Work **Partners**

A group of stars that looks like an animal or another object is called a constellation. In your dictionary, you can see the constellation called The Big Dipper. What other constellations do you know? Make a diagram of a constellation you know.

Word Study

Think of creative ways to write vocabulary words to help you remember their meanings. Here are three examples:

Mountain   Orbit   Canyon

Garden

A **Complete the sentences.**

1. Most flowers grow from _____seeds_____.

2. Other flowers grow from _____. You plant them in the fall, and they come up the next spring or summer.

3. _____ go into the soil and bring water to the plant.

4. _____ is an example of an evergreen tree. It is green all year.

5. Many commercial flower growers start seeds in a _____.

6. Most trees have a strong central _____.

7. Many _____ grow from the trunk.

8. In the fall, _____ turn colors and fall from the trees.

9. In a pine tree, the seeds are found in the _____.

⌐ Grammar Connection: Giving Directions: *First, Next, Then,* •⌐
After that, Finally

Note:
• Use *First* to give the beginning step.
• Use *Next, Then, and After that* for some of the new steps in the directions.
• Use *Finally* for the last step.

B **Put the directions for *How to Start a Garden* in order from 1 to 6. In your note-book, put the sentences in a paragraph. Begin each sentence with one of the order words.**

_____ Enjoy your garden. Remember to cut some flowers for your table.

_____ Prepare the soil. Clear all the weeds and add mulch and compost.

_____ Water your garden regularly.

_____ Plant your seeds and small plants, carefully following all directions.

__1__ Choose the area for your garden and design the garden on paper.

_____ Buy the seeds and the plants that you like.

C Look at the picture of the garden in your dictionary. Write the color of each flower.

1. _____red_____ roses   5. _____ daisies

2. _____ lilies   6. _____ irises

3. _____ marigolds   7. _____ chrysanthemums

4. _____ geraniums   8. _____ daffodils

D Write the name of the tree for each leaf or seed.

| pine tree | elm tree | maple tree | ~~oak tree~~ |

1. __oak tree__   2. _____   3. _____   4. _____

CD 3
Track 7

E Listen to the description of each flower. Write the number of the flower under the correct picture.

a.   b.   c.   d.   e.

_____   _____   _____   _____   __1__

Word Work Partners

Discuss or write the answers to the questions.

1. Do you ever buy flowers for anyone? What is the occasion?
2. What kind of flowers do you sometimes buy for your house?
3. What flower would you like to receive for your birthday?
4. Do you have a garden? What flowers do you grow?

Desert

A Circle the correct answer.

1. Which animal is more dangerous: (a scorpion) or a grasshopper?

2. Which animal can be poisonous: a snake or a moth?

3. Which has eight legs: a spider or a fly?

4. Which animal moves more slowly: a rat or a tortoise?

5. Which animal lives longer: a coyote or a tortoise?

6. Which insect can jump: an ant or a grasshopper?

7. Which animal can attack people: a mountain lion or a camel?

8. Which insect stings: a cricket or a scorpion?

Grammar Connection: Simple Present Tense – Questions

What	**does**	a mountain lion	**eat?**
What	**do**	mountain lions	**eat?**

Note:
- Use *does* or *do* after the *Wh-* question word.
- Use the base form of the verb after the subject.

B Complete the questions for the underlined answers.

1. Where ___do mountain lions live_____?

   Mountain lions live in North and South America.

2. How long _____?

   Mountain lions from ten to twenty years.

3. How much _____?

   An adult male weighs from 115 to 200 pounds.

4. When _____?

   Mountain lions hunt at night.

5. What _____?

   Mountain lions eat deer, sheep, and other smaller animals.

6. How many cubs _____

A female has from two to six cubs.

7. How long _____?

The cubs live with their mother for between one and two years.

C **Match the words and their definitions.**

_g_ **1.** sand dune

a. a small rock

____ **2.** boulder

b. a place in the desert with water and trees

____ **3.** oasis

c. a tree with no branches and with large leaves at the top

____ **4.** palm tree

d. an area with little rain

____ **5.** desert

e. a large rock

____ **6.** pebble

f. a green desert plant that sometimes has needles

____ **7.** cactus

g. a hill of sand

CD 3
Track 8

D **Listen to each conversation between two people at a zoo. Then, read each statement and circle *T* for true or *F* for false.**

1. Tortoises live in the water.   T   (F)

2. Tortoises can grow to five feet long.   T   F

3. Many animals attack tortoises.   T   F

4. Tortoises eat insects such as flies.   T   F

5. Tortoises have strong teeth.   T   F

6. There are more than 135 species of owls.   T   F

7. Owls sleep at night.   T   F

8. Owls eat insects and small birds.   T   F

9. Owls move their eyes from side to side.   T   F

10. Owls have ears.   T   F

Word Work **Partners**

Write a description of one of the animals in the desert. Don't write the name of the animal in your description. Read your description to the class. Can the other students guess the animal?

Rain Forest

A Write the words in the correct group.

chimpanzee	hummingbird	wasp	peacock	butterfly
aardvark	monkey	parakeet	alligator	beetle
caterpillar	flamingo	tarantula	gorilla	parrot

Animals	Birds	Insects
chimpanzee	_____	_____
_____	_____	_____
_____	_____	_____
_____	_____	_____
_____	_____	_____

Grammar Connection: Comparative Adjectives

A gorilla is **larger than** a monkey.
A monkey is **noisier than** a crocodile.
A tarantula is **more dangerous than** a beetle.

Note:
- Comparative adjectives compare two people, places, or things.
- For one-syllable adjectives, add *er* + *than*.
- For two-syllable adjectives ending in *y*, change the *y* to *i* and add *er* + *than*.
- For other adjectives with two or more syllables, add *more than* before the adjective.

B Complete the sentences with the comparative form of the adjective.

1. A frog is (loud) _____louder than_____ an aardvark.

2. A parrot is (colorful) _____ a flamingo.

3. Crocodiles are (heavy) _____ alligators.

4. A tiger is (strong) _____ a panther.

5. Chimpanzees are (intelligent) _____ monkeys.

6. A butterfly is (pretty) _____ a caterpillar.

7. An aardvark is (quiet) _____ than an orangutan.

8. A panther is (fast) _____ a tiger.

9. A tarantula is (frightening) _____ a beetle.

10. A monkey is (small) _____ an orangutan.

C Look at the picture of the rain forest. Complete the sentences.

1. The _____monkey_____ has a long tail. It's climbing a tree.

2. The _____ spends most of its life in trees. It's holding a vine.

3. The _____ is part of the cat family. It's orange with black stripes.

4. The _____ and the _____ spend most of the

   day swimming in the water or lying on a riverbank.

5. The _____ has a long nose. It can dig deep into the ground to

   find ants and other insects.

D Write the name of each animal.

1. _____   2. _____   3. _____

4. _____   5. _____   6. _____

E Listen to each statement. Write the name of the correct bird or animal from Exercise D.

CD 3
Track 9

1. _____parrot_____   4. _____

2. _____   5. _____

3. _____   6. _____

Word Work **Partners**

Would you like to own a parrot or a parakeet? Write two advantages and two
disadvantages to owning a pet bird.

Grasslands

A   **Complete the paragraph.**

There are large areas of grasslands on most of the continents. Trees provide a home

for birds and insects, such as _____sparrows_____ and _____.

Tall animals, such as _____, eat leaves from the taller trees. Some

animals, such as _____, spend most of the day in or near water

holes. The grass provides food for many animals. The tall grass hides some of the

smaller animals, such as _____ and _____. Some

animals, such as _____, live in tunnels under the ground.

Grammar Connection: Superlative Adjectives

> A giraffe is **the tallest** animal.
> An elephant is **the heaviest** animal.
> A hippopotamus is **the most aggressive** animal.

Note:
- Remember that superlative adjectives compare three or more people, places, or things.

B   **Complete each sentence about the grassland animals in your dictionary with the superlative form of the adjective.**

1. An ostrich is (large) _____the largest_____ bird.

2. An antelope has (long) _____ horns.

3. A koala is (slow) _____ animal.

4. An elephant is (intelligent) _____ animal.

5. A cheetah (fast) _____ animal.

6. A lion is (dangerous) _____ animal.

7. A gopher is (small) _____ animal.

8. A rhinoceros is (strong) _____ animal.

9. A bee is (beneficial) _____ insect in the world.

C Complete the sentences.

1. _____A giraffe_____ is very tall and has a long neck.

2. _____ has tusks and a long trunk.

3. _____ looks like a horse with stripes.

4. _____ has long antlers.

5. _____ has a mane and a long tail.

6. _____ has two short horns on its face.

7. _____ has two strong back legs and can hop long distances.

8. _____ has long fur and two horns on its head.

9. The hard foot of a mammal is _____. The soft foot of a mammal

   is _____.

CD 3
Track 10

D Listen to the information about five endangered animals. Check the reasons why the number of these animals is decreasing.

Loss of habitat - The population of the world is growing. People need the land for homes and for growing food, so there is less land for animals.

Hunter - This is a person who looks for and kills animals for sport or for food.

Poacher – This is a person who hunts animals illegally.

	Loss of habitat	Hunters	Ranchers and farmers	Poachers
Rhinoceros	✓	_____	_____	✓
Elephant	_____	_____	_____	_____
Cheetah	_____	_____	_____	_____
Kangaroo	_____	_____	_____	_____
Zebra	_____	_____	_____	_____

Word Work Partners

Write five questions about animals that live in the grasslands.

Ask another group your questions.

Examples: **Which animal has two long legs and a long neck?**

Which animal has black and white stripes?

Polar Lands

A **Complete the sentences. You will use some words more than once.**

wings	beak	claws	tusks
flippers	antlers	~~whiskers~~	fur

1. An animal's _____whiskers_____ protect its face.

2. An animal uses its _____ to fly.

3. An animal's _____ protects it from the cold.

4. An animal can fight with its _____ or its _____.

5. A bird uses its _____ or _____ to hold things.

6. An animal uses its _____ to swim.

7. A bird uses its _____ to open, tear, and eat food.

Grammar Connection: *Too* and *So*

Statement	Too	So
A wolf **is** a mammal.	A fox **is, too.**	**So is** a fox.
A walrus **has** flippers.	A seal **does, too.**	**So does** a seal.
Penguins **have** beaks.	Reindeer **do, too.**	**So do** reindeer.
A polar bear **can** swim long distances.	A moose **can, too.**	**So can** a moose.

Note:
* Statements with *too* or *so* mean *also* or *in addition*.
* In these sentences and responses, the verb and the auxiliary agree.
* Put the auxiliary after *so*, then put the subject.

B **Write a statement with *too* or *so*. Use the word in parentheses.**

1. A fox hunts smaller animals. (a wolf) __A wolf does, too.__ or __So does a wolf.__

2. A moose has antlers. (a reindeer) _____

3. Geese fly south in the winter. (falcons) _____

4. A walrus is a social animal. (a penguin) _____

5. A penguin can dive deep underwater. (a seal) _____

6. Bears eat meat. (wolves) _____

7. A reindeer eats plants. (a moose) _____

8. A fox can hunt quietly. (a wolf) _____

9. Polar bears are endangered animals. (Arctic foxes) _____

C **Complete the sentences with the name of the animal.**

goose	~~polar bear~~	reindeer
penguin	falcon	whale

1. _____A polar bear_____ is one of the largest polar animals. It lives at sea half the time and on land the other half. It can walk up to forty miles a day.

2. _____ is a bird, but it cannot fly. It has flippers instead of wings. This animal lives in large groups, which can have 10,000 members or more.

3. _____ lives in the Arctic in the summer and then flies south for the winter.

4. _____ lives in the ocean, but it is not a fish. It is the largest mammal in the world. It must come to the surface to breathe air.

5. _____ has brown fur, but its neck and tail are white. It is a fast runner and an excellent swimmer. This animal lives in large herds of 1,000 or more.

6. _____ is the fastest bird in the world. It has very good eyes and can see food on the ground from a mile away.

CD 3
Track 11

D **Listen to descriptions of these four animals. Write the number of the description under the correct animal.**

a. ____   b. ____   c. ____   d. ____

Word Work Small Group

Polar animals live in difficult conditions. It's cold most of the year in the Arctic. For many months, there is little or no sunlight. Snow covers the ground most of the year. How do polar bears survive in these conditions?

Sea

A Write the name of the correct sea animal under each picture.

1. _____crab_____ 2. _____ 3. _____ 4. _____

5. _____ 6. _____ 7. _____ 8. _____

Grammar Connection: Statements with *Both*

Both a dolphin **and** a whale are mammals.
Both a cod **and** a bass have scales.

Note:
- *Both* means the one and the other together.
- Use the plural form of the verb with *both*. Other parts of the sentence may need the plural form, also.

B Combine the two statements with *both*.

1. A crab has a shell. A shrimp has a shell.

   Both a crab and a shrimp have shells.

2. A sailfish swims fast. A swordfish swims fast.

   _____

3. A starfish moves slowly. A sea horse moves slowly.

   _____

4. A shark has sharp teeth. An eel has sharp teeth.

   _____

5. A jellyfish can sting a person. A sea anemone can sting a person.

_____

6. A dolphin can jump out of the water. A sailfish can jump out of the water.

_____

C **Write the names of four more sea creatures in each group.**

A <u>vertebrate</u> is an animal with a skeleton.

An <u>invertebrate</u> is an animal without bones. It has a soft body.

Vertebrates	Invertebrates
shark	octopus
tuna	sea anemone
_____	_____
_____	_____
_____	_____
_____	_____

CD 3
Track 12

D **The ocean is very deep. Listen and draw a line from each ocean creature to the depth at which it usually swims.**

| Word Work | Small Group |

Discuss or write your answers.

1. You are a fisherman. Which fish would you like to catch?

2. You are a scuba diver. Which fish would you like to see?

3. You are a scientist. Which fish would you like to study?

4. You are a film director. Which fish would you like to make a documentary about?

Woodlands

┌─ **Grammar Connection:** *Yes/No* **Questions and Answers** ─┐

Questions	Affirmative	Negative
Is it large?	**Yes**, it **is**.	**No**, it **isn't**.
Can it fly?	**Yes**, it **can**.	**No**, it **can't**.
Does it build a nest?	**Yes**, it **does**.	**No**, it **doesn't**.

Note:
• Use the same auxiliary verb in both the question and the answer.

A One student is trying to guess the correct animal on this page. Complete the answers to the *Yes/No* questions. Can you guess the animal?

1. Is it a bird?   No, ___it___ ___isn't___.

2. Is it an insect?   No, _____ _____.

3. Is it a mammal?   Yes, _____ _____.

4. Can it hop?   No, _____ _____.

5. Does it climb trees?   No, _____ _____.

6. Does it have a long tail?   Yes, _____ _____.

7. Is it black?   Yes, _____ _____.

8. Does it have a white stripe?   Yes, _____ _____.

9. Is it a _____?   Yes, _____. You guessed it!

B Write the name of the correct woodland animal.

1. This long, thin animal is usually pink or gray. It lives in the ground. It is a favorite food for birds. ___worm___

2. This small animal has a furry tail. It can run up and down trees and jump from branch to branch. It collects nuts. _____

3. This bird has a long, sharp beak. It sits on a branch and makes holes in trees.

   _____

4. This large bird is the largest hunting bird. It uses its sharp claws to catch smaller animals. _____

5. This large woodland animal spends its day eating leaves, flowers, and fruit. The males grow antlers. _____

6. This animal lives in rivers and lakes. It can cut down trees with its strong front teeth. It builds its home, called a dam, in the water. _____

7. This animal walks slowly through the woods. The other animals do not bother it because sharp needles, called quills, cover its body. _____

8. This small animal is black with a white stripe on its back. When it thinks it is in danger, it gives off a terrible smell. _____

CD 3
Track 13

C **Listen to the description of each animal. Write the number of the description under the correct animal.**

a.	b.	c.	d.	e.

_____   _____   <u>1</u>   _____   _____

Word Work Small Group

Discuss or write the answers to these questions.
1. Which of these woodland animals live in your area?
2. Are any of these animals a problem in your area? Why?
3. Which of these animals will eat the vegetables in your garden?
4. Which of these animals live in the ground?
5. Which of these animals build nests in trees?

Word Study

Put vocabulary words into groups or categories. In this unit, you could classify animals several ways. For example:
1.   Animals that run—Animals that swim—Animals that fly
2.   Insects—Birds—Fish

Another way to classify words is to decide on one group and find several words that belong in that group, such as:
1.   Animals that are dangerous
2.   Animals that live in my country
3.   Animals that are larger than I am

Math

A Complete the chart. Write the verb and the operation.

Sign	Verb	Operation	Example
+	_____add_____	_____addition_____	10 + 5 = 15
−	_____	_____	10 − 5 = 5
×	_____	_____	10 × 5 = 50
÷	_____	_____	10 ÷ 5 = 2

B Read the problem. Write the numbers and solve the problems.

1. Add 6 and 12.   _____6 + 12 = 18_____

2. Subtract 7 from 15.   _____

3. Divide 20 by 5.   _____

4. Multiply 3 by 5.   _____

5. What is 5 times 6?   _____

Grammar Connection: **Math Problems with *How much* and *What***

How much What	is	seven **plus** ten? twenty **minus** five? six **times** three? six **multiplied by** three? eight **divided by** two?

C Write the math problem beginning with *How much* or *What*.

1. 2 + 8   _____How much is two plus eight?_____

2. 12 − 5   _____

3. 3 × 5   _____

4. 7 + 14 + 9   _____

5. 18 ÷ 2   _____

6. 10 × 4   _____

7. 20 − 10   _____

8. 12 × 5   _____

9. 30 ÷ 2   _____

D Write the name of an object that is the same shape as each shape or solid.

circle   oval   rectangle   triangle

__clock__   _____   _____   _____

sphere   cube   cone   cylinder

_____   _____   _____   _____

E Complete the sentences about each figure.

1.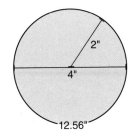

The _____radius_____ of the circle is 2".

The _____ is 4".

The _____ is 12.56".

2.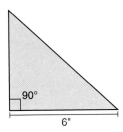

The _____ of the triangle is 6".

The _____ is 90°.

3.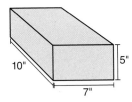

The _____ of the figure is 5".

The _____ is 7".

The _____ is 10".

CD 3
Track 14

F Listen to each word problem. Write the numbers and solve the problem. What operation did you use?

1. _____$.99 × 5 = $4.95_____   Operation: _____multiplication_____

2. _____   Operation: _____

3. _____   Operation: _____

4. _____   Operation: _____

5. _____   Operation: _____

Word Work Small Group

Write three math problems. Read each problem to your group. Your classmates will solve the problems.

Science

A **Match each picture with the correct description.**

1.  **2.**  **3.**

4.  **5.**  **6.**

___5___ **a.** The scientist is pouring liquid into a flask. He is using a funnel.

_____ **b.** The scientist is dropping liquid into a petri dish.

_____ **c.** The scientist is holding a beaker and a test tube.

_____ **d.** The scientist is looking into a microscope.

_____ **e.** The scientist is pouring liquid into a graduated cylinder. She is using a funnel.

_____ **f.** The scientist is pouring liquid from a beaker into a flask.

B **Complete the sentences.**

1. Use a _____funnel_____ to help pour liquids into a flask.

2. Put a _____ on top of a flask.

3. Use a _____ to heat liquids or solids.

4. Use _____ to pick up small objects.

5. Use a _____ to examine small objects.

6. Put a _____ or a _____ under the microscope.

7. Use a _____ to separate light.

8. Use a _____ to pick up metal objects, such as iron and steel.

Grammar Connection: **Definitions**

Physics is the science that studies energy and matter.
A flask is a glass container with a long, narrow neck.

Note:
• A definition gives the meaning of a word.

C **Match the word and the definition.**

_____ **1.** chemistry

_____ **2.** biology

_____ **3.** Bunsen burner

_____ **4.** test tube

_____ **5.** element

_____ **6.** atom

_____ **7.** balance

_____ **8.** prism

a. the science that studies elements, atoms, and molecules

b. a gas burner for heating chemicals

c. a thin glass tube used in science experiments

d. the smallest unit of matter

e. the science that studies living things

f. a glass that separates light into colors

g. a basic chemical substance

h. a scale that compares the weight of two things

CD 3
Track 15

D **Listen to the science lab instructions. Write the number of the statement under the correct picture.**

a.

_____

b.

_____

c.

_____

d.

_____

e.

_____

f.

_____

g.

1

h.

_____

Word Work **Small Group**

Draw three items you can find in a science lab. Your
partners will try to guess the piece of equipment you drew.

Writing

A Put the steps for writing an essay in the correct order.

_____ **a.** She wrote an outline with her best ideas.

_____ **b.** Yolanda brainstormed different ideas. She crossed out some of them.

_____ **c.** Yolanda showed the draft of her essay to two other students and got their feedback.

__1__ **d.** The teacher assigned the students an essay topic.

_____ **e.** Yolanda typed her essay.

_____ **f.** Yolanda wrote her first draft. She concentrated on her ideas and organization.

_____ **g.** Yolanda handed in her essay on the due date.

_____ **h.** Yolanda edited her essay. She made her ideas clearer, corrected grammar errors, and checked the punctuation.

Grammar Connection: Past Statements with *already* and *yet*

She wrote an outline **already**.
She **already** wrote an outline.
She didn't write an outline **yet**.

Note:
- Use *already* in affirmative statements. Place *already* at the end of a sentence or before the verb.
- Use *yet* in negative sentences. Place *yet* at the end of the sentence.

B Answer the questions with *already* or *yet*.

1. Did Justin write a draft of his essay?

    ___Yes, he wrote a draft already.___ or ___No, he didn't write a draft yet.___

2. Did Marco get feedback from another student?

    Yes, _____

3. Did Sofia edit her essay?

    No, _____

4. Did George check his punctuation?

    No, _____

5. Did Lia type her final draft?

Yes, _____

6. Did David hand in his paper?

No, _____

c Read the sentences. Correct the capitalization and add the missing punctuation. Then, complete the punctuation rules.

1. a dictionary gives the definitions of many words

   a. Begin the sentence with a _____*capital*_____ letter.

   b. Put a _____ at the end of the sentence.

2. The teacher said open your dictionaries.

   a. Put a _____ after the word *said.*

   b. Begin the word *open* with a _____ letter.

   c. Put _____ around the words of the teacher.

3. What kind of dictionary do you have

   a. Put a _____ at the end of the sentence.

4. Wonderful

   a. Put an _____ at the end of the sentence.

D Listen and write the sentences you hear. Use the correct punctuation.

CD 3
Track 16

1. What time is it? _____

2. _____

3. _____

4. _____

5. _____

6. _____

7. _____

Word Work **Partners**

With a partner, check the punctuation of the sentences you wrote in Exercise D.
Label each punctuation mark you used.

Explore, Rule, Invent

A **Complete the sentences. Use the verb in the past tense.**

1. The company _introduced_ a faster computer.

2. The space ship _____ the moon.

3. Astronauts _____ the surface of the moon.

4. The soldiers _____ the country.

5. The citizens _____ the president.

6. The scientist _____ a cure for the disease.

7. The workers _____ a bridge across the river.

8. The jet _____ around the world.

9. The boat _____ across the ocean.

10. The soldiers went home when the war _____.

11. A dictator _____ the country.

12. The factory _____ electronic equipment.

defend
build
~~introduce~~
end
reach
dicoover
fly
explore
rule
sail
produce
elect

Grammar Connection: **Professions Ending with -r, -er, -or**

Verb	Noun
explore	explorer
sail	sailor
drive	driver

Note:
- In English, the name of many jobs is based on the verb.
- Add -r, -er, or -or to these verb to form the job or profession.

B **Write the job for each verb.**

Verb	Job		Verb	Job
1. explore	_explorer_		7. invent	_____
2. compose	_____		8. teach	_____
3. sail	_____		9. rule	_____
4. paint	_____		10. drive	_____
5. edit	_____		11. produce	_____
6. act	_____		12. assemble	_____

C **Match the person, country, or company and the achievement.**

_e_ **1.** Ferdinand Magellan

_____ **2.** Charles Lindbergh

_____ **3.** Karl Benz

_____ **4.** Galileo Galilei

_____ **5.** Marie Curie

_____ **6.** Russia

_____ **7.** The Chunnel

_____ **8.** Wolfgang Amadeus Mozart

_____ **9.** Mao Zedong

_____ **10.** Mother Teresa

a. builtt the first automobile.

b. composed *Don Giovanni* and *The Magic Flute.*

c. flew solo across the Atlantic Ocean.

d. ruled China for more than 25 years.

e. sailed around the world.

f. won the Nobel Peace Prize.

g. launched the first space station.

h. discovered radium.

i. opened between England and France in 1994.

j. invented the telescope.

CD 3
Track 17

D **Listen to the description of each event. Write the number of the description under the correct picture.**

a. _____ b. _____ c. _____ d. _1_

e. _____ f. _____ g. _____ h. _____

Word Work **Small Group**

As a group, list five important inventions. Try to put them in order. Which item was invented first, second, third, etc.?

U.S. Government and Citizenship

A A person who wants to become a citizen of the United States must pass a citizenship test. Match the questions and answers to some of the questions.

_c_ **1.** What are the colors of the flag?

____ **2.** How many stars are on the flag?

____ **3.** What does each star mean?

____ **4.** When is Independence Day celebrated?

____ **5.** In what month do citizens vote for president?

____ **6.** Where does the president live?

____ **7.** Who elects the Congress?

a. one is for each state

b. July 4th

c. red, white, and blue

d. in the White House

e. fifty

f. the people

g. November

Grammar Connection: **Present Perfect Tense**

I You We They	**have**	(never)	**voted.** **spoken** with my congressman. **demonstrated.**
He She	**has**		

Note:
- Use the present perfect tense to talk about an indefinite time in the past. If you talk about a specific time, use the past tense.
- Form the present perfect tense with *have* or *has* + the past participle.

B Complete the statements with *have* or *has*.

1. I _____ *have* _____ never met a senator from my state.

2. We _____ visited the White House twice.

3. He _____ never taken a tour of the Capitol Building.

4. They _____ voted.

5. She _____ served on a jury.

6. They _____ protested against the war several times.

7. He _____ never served in the army.

C Complete the sentences about the U.S. government.

1. The legislative branch of the government is called _____Congress_____.

2. Congress meets in the _____.

3. The 435 members of the House of Representatives are called

   _____ and _____.

4. The 100 members of the Senate are called _____.

5. The executive branch is the president and _____.

6. There are nine _____ on the Supreme Court.

7. All _____ can vote for the president every four years.

8. On their ballot, people choose the _____ they want.

CD 3
Track 18

D Listen to each question and answer. Then, check *Citizen, Permanent Resident,* or both.

citizen—a person who was born in the United States or who has become a naturalized citizen

permanent resident—a person who was born in another country and who applied to live permanently in the United States

	Citizen	Permanent Resident
1. Does everyone have to obey the law?	✓	✓
2. Can everyone vote for president?	____	____
3. Does everyone have to pay taxes?	____	____
4. Can everyone serve on a jury?	____	____
5. Can everyone protest?	____	____
6. Can everyone serve in the military?	____	____

Word Study

One of the best ways to remember vocabulary words is to write sentences using the words. Write sentences that are true and that relate to your life.

Examples:

The president of my country is _____.

Scientists are trying to discover a cure for cancer.

The periodic table is on the wall in my chemistry class.

201

Fine Arts

A **Complete the sentences.**

1. A _____portrait_____ is a painting of a person.

2. A _____ is a painting of an outdoor scene.

3. An artist will often make a _____ of a scene before painting it.

4. Before painting, an artist puts the paint on a _____.

5. An artist sets the canvas on an _____.

6. A person who sits for a painting is a _____.

7. People put a _____ around the edges of a completed painting.

┌ **Grammar Connection: *How do you like ... ?*** ─────────────────

How do you like	this painting? this pottery?	I like it a lot. It's beautiful! I like it very much. I love the colors.	I don't like it very much. Well, it's different. What is it?

Note:
• Use *How do you like* to ask someone's opinion.

B **Ask for an opinion about each painting. Answer with an expression from the chart or write a different opinion.**

1. __How do you like this painting?__

   _____

   _____

2. _____

   _____

   _____

3. _____

   _____

c Write the correct response to each question.

He's a sculptor.	It's the countryside in the winter.
~~I like modern art.~~	That's my daughter.
It's a vase of flowers.	He uses clay.
It's on the side of the building.	He uses oil paint.

1. What kind of art do you like? _____ I like modern art. _____

2. What kind of paint does he use? _____

3. What kind of artist is he? _____

4. What material does he use? _____

5. What is that a still life of? _____

6. What is that a landscape of? _____

7. Who is that a portrait of? _____

8. Where is the mural? _____

D Write the names of two kinds of equipment or materials that each artist uses.

1. photographer: _____ _____

2. painter: _____ _____

3. sculptor: _____ _____

E Listen to the four conversations in a museum. Write the type of art that each visitor wants to see. Then, write the name of the correct section of the museum.

CD 3
Track 19

	Art	Section		Art	Section
1.	modern art	C	3.	_____	___
2.	_____	___	4.	_____	___

Word Work Small Group

Discuss the answers to these questions about art.
1. Do you have any paintings or posters on your walls at home?
2. What are the paintings of ? (flowers / landscapes / portraits) Who is the painter?
3. Do you take photographs of your family or your vacations?
4. What do you do with the photographs?

Performing Arts

A Write one type of performance for each performer.

1. dancers: _____ballet_____

2. actors: _____

3. singers: _____

4. singers and backup singers: _____

5. musicians and conductor: _____

B Read the statement. Circle *T* if the statement is true. Circle *F* if the statement is false.

1. You buy tickets at the box office.   (T)   F

2. Actors usually perform on a stage.   T   F

3. The conductor leads the orchestra.   T   F

4. After a performance, the audience bows.   T   F

5. In an opera, the performers sing.   T   F

6. At a rock concert, there are spotlights on the singers.   T   F

7. The backup singers stand at the front of the stage.   T   F

Grammar Connection: Adjective Clauses with *who*

A drummer is a person **who plays the drums.**
An usher is a person **who shows people their seats.**

Note:
* An adjective clause describes a noun.
* Use *who* to refer to people.

C Complete the adjective clauses about the performers.

1. An actor is _____a person who acts in a movie or play_____.

2. A conductor is _____.

3. A guitarist is _____.

4. A singer is _____.

5. A dancer is _____.

D Complete the information.

Would you like to see a symphony orchestra? First, buy your _____tickets_____ at the box office or online. On the day of the performance, arrive early. The usher will give you a _____ and then show you to your _____. You will see the orchestra on the _____.

When the _____ enters, the _____ will applaud. The conductor will signal for silence. Then, the _____ will begin to play. There is often a solo by a well-known _____. When the concert is over, the audience will _____. The conductor and musicians will _____.

E Listen to each speaker talk about a performance he or she attended. Write the number of the conversation next to the correct performance.

CD 3
Track 20

_____ **a.** ballet

_____ **b.** rock concert

_____ **c.** symphony orchestra

_____ **d.** play

Word Work Small Group

Write the name of a popular performer or group.

Rock group: _____

Singer: _____

Actor: _____   Actress: _____

Dancer: _____

Symphony orchestra: _____

Instruments

He She	**has been**	**practicing** **playing**	the piano	for two hours. since 9:00.

Note:

• The present perfect progressive tense talks about an action that started in the past and continues in the present time.

A Write a sentence about each performer using the present perfect progressive tense. How long has each person been performing or practicing?

1.

She has been playing the trumpet for ten minutes.

2.

3.

4.

5.

_____

6.

_____

B Write the name of two instruments that are found in each section of an orchestra.

1. the brass section: _____ *trombone* _____   _____

2. the string section: _____   _____

3. the percussion section: _____   _____

4. the keyboard section: _____   _____

5. the woodwind section: _____   _____

C Listen and write the name of the instrument you hear.

CD 3
Track 21

1. _____ a harmonica _____   **6.** _____

2. _____   **7.** _____

3. _____   **8.** _____

4. _____   **9.** _____

5. _____   **10.** _____

Word Work Small Group

Describe one instrument that is popular in your country but is not pictured on these pages. Draw a picture of the instrument. In which section would you find this instrument?

Film, TV, and Music

A Write the type of film or TV program you can associate with these words.

1. funny, laugh: _____comedy_____

2. detective, crime: _____

3. score, baseball: _____

4. bulletin, update: _____

5. love, boyfriend: _____

6. prize, contestants: _____

7. cowboys, Indians: _____

8. scary, monster: _____

Grammar Connection: *I would rather / I'd rather*

I would I'd	rather	**see** a mystery. **watch** a game show. **listen** to some rock.

Note:
- I *would rather* means *I would prefer*.
- Use the base form of the verb after *rather*.
- Use *I'd rather* in conversation.

B Respond to each suggestion with a different choice. Begin with *I'd rather*.

1. Let's see a western. _____*I'd rather see a comedy.*_____

2. Let's watch a game show. _____

3. Let's see a fantasy. _____

4. Let's listen to some jazz. _____

5. Let's watch a documentary. _____

6. Let's watch a soap opera. _____

7. Let's listen to some rock. _____

c Read the short review of each film. Then, match the kind of film with each description. Write the number of the review next to the kind of film.

1. Each night, another person disappears in the village of Rockport.

2. Two people meet on vacation and fall in love.

3. The body of a young man is found in an art museum. Who killed him and why?

4. A look at global warming and its effects on the planet.

5. Will rescuers reach the damaged cruise ship before it sinks?

6. A spaceship from a distant planet attacks Earth.

a. Documentary ____   d. Action   ____

b. Science fiction ____   e. Mystery   ____

c. Romance ____   f. Horror   _1_

CD 3
Track 22

D Listen to these lines from TV programs. On which type of TV program will you hear these lines?

____ a. children's program   _1_ d. news

____ b. game show   ____ e. nature program

____ c. soap opera   ____ f. talk show

Word Work **Small Group**

Discuss or write your answers to these questions about music.
1. What kind of music do you enjoy?
2. Who is your favorite singer?
3. What is your favorite group?

Word Study

Use other sources to help you learn and practice vocabulary words.
- If you have the dictionary or the workbook CDs, listen to them at home. Repeat the words and sentences.
- If you have access to the Internet, visit the websites of museums and read about a famous artist in English.
- If you enjoy music, buy a CD of your favorite music with English lyrics.
- If you live in an English-speaking country, read the TV guide of a newspaper in English.

Beach

A **Complete the sentences.**

1. _____motorboat_____ pulls a water-skier.

2. _____ shows ships that they are near a dangerous area.

3. The surfers are happy today because the _____ are big.

4. It's very sunny. _____ sunscreen on your face and back.

5. My children can't swim well, so they wear _____.

6. You can breathe and see underwater if you wear a _____

   and a _____.

Grammar Connection: Tense Contrast

Present Progressive Tense	The man **is swimming**.
Simple Present Tense	The man **swims** every day.
Future Tense	The man **is going to swim** tomorrow.
Past Tense	The nurse **swam** for an hour yesterday.

B **Complete the sentences about the beach with the correct form of the verb.**

1. The lifeguard is standing. He (watch) _____ the swimmers.

2. The little boy (finish) _____ the sandcastle a few minutes ago.

3. He (go) _____ in the water after his mother puts on sunscreen.

4. The little boy and his mother (come) _____ to the beach every day.

5. The woman is reading. In a little while, she (swim) _____.

6. The woman in the red bathing suit is tired because she (surf)

   _____ all morning.

7. The motorboat (pull) _____ the water-skier.

8. The sailboarder always (wear) _____ a life jacket.

9. When I was a child, we (go) _____ to the beach every summer.

10. We (not go) _____ to the beach anymore because we

   (not live) _____ near the ocean.

C **Complete the advertisement about this beach resort. Circle the correct word.**

Enjoy a week in the sun at beautiful Laguna Beach Resort.

1. [(Swim)   Wave] in one of our three pools.

2. Walk on one of our beautiful [fins   sand] beaches.

3. Open a book and relax in one of our comfortable [beach chairs   snorkels].

4. Fish from our ocean [pier   life jacket].

5. Rent one of our many [sailboats   swimmers].

6. Take a [shovel   surfing] lesson.

7. Your children will enjoy the Kids Program. There is a [sand castle   water wing] building contest and a [seashell   cooler] hunt. There is always a [sunbather lifeguard] on duty to watch the children in the water.

8. Put on a mask and [snorkel   shovel] to explore life under the sea.

D **In your notebook, write about each picture. What is each person doing?**

1.   2.   3.

CD 3
Track 23

E **Listen. Check the items that this family is bringing to the beach.**

✓ surfboard	___ beach ball	___ towels
___ cooler	___ sunscreen	___ snorkel
___ water wings	___ umbrella	___ fins
___ pail and shovel	___ beach chairs	___ mask

Word Work **Partners**

You are going to stay at a beach resort for five days. Write five sentences about what you plan to do.

Camping

A Who uses each piece of equipment? Write the name of the correct person under each picture.

1. _a rock climber_

2. _____

3. _____

4. _____

5. _____

6. _____

Grammar Connection: Statements with *so*

| I forgot the matches, | so I couldn't light the campfire. |
| I forgot my sleeping bag, | so I had to sleep on the hard ground. |

Note:
- *So* connects the two parts of the sentence.
- *So* shows the result of an action.

B Match the two parts of the sentences.

_d_ 1. I forgot my fishing pole,   **a.** so I couldn't cook dinner.

____ 2. I forgot the lantern,   **b.** so I was thirsty on my hike.

____ 3. I forgot the camping stove,   **c.** so I couldn't see in the dark.

____ 4. I forgot the insect repellent,   **d.** so I couldn't go fishing.

____ 5. I forgot the compass,   **e.** so I couldn't go rock climbing.

____ 6. I forgot the paddle,   **f.** so the bugs bit me all day.

____ 7. I forgot my canteen,   **g.** so I got lost.

____ 8. I forgot my rope,   **h.** so I couldn't use the canoe.

C Complete the story of this camping trip.

My friends and I took a ten-day trip along the Colorado River through the Grand Canyon. We traveled in [rafts   tents]. At times, the river was calm. Other times, we had to use our [compasses   paddles] to control the raft. We [camped   drove] next to the river. It only took a few minutes to set up our [tents   ropes]. In the afternoons, some people [hiked   swam] in the river. Other people hiked up different [maps   trails]. At night, we cooked our food on a [camping stove   lantern]. After dinner, we sat around the [canoe   campfire] and talked. Sleeping was very comfortable because we had both [fishing poles   air mattresses] and [sleeping bags   canteens].

CD 3
Track 24

D Listen as a man and a woman pack their backpacks for a camping trip. Circle who will carry each piece of equipment, the man (*M*), the woman (*W*), or both.

1. camping stove   Ⓜ   W   7. fishing pole   M   W

2. matches   M   W   8. sleeping bag   M   W

3. food   M   W   9. air mattress   M   W

4. trail map   M   W   10. tent   M   W

5. pocket knife   M   W   11. canteen   M   W

6. compass   M   W   12. insect repellent   M   W

Word Work Small Group

Discuss or write about different locations in your area.
1. I can camp at _____.
2. I can hike in _____.
3. I can rent a canoe or raft at _____.
4. I can fish in _____.

City Park

A Write the correct verb. You can use a verb more than once.

| fly | watch | ride | climb | walk | sit |

1. ___ride___ a carousel
2. _____ on the jungle gym
3. _____ a bicycle
4. _____ a puppet show
5. _____ across the bridge

6. _____ on the monkey bars
7. _____ at a picnic table
8. _____ on the path
9. _____ a Ferris wheel
10. _____ a kite

B Complete the words.

1. monkey _____
2. _____ show
3. _____ can

4. jungle _____
5. amusement _____
6. roller _____

Grammar Connection: Past Progressive Tense

I You He/She	**was**	**playing** in the sandbox. **riding** on the carousel. **having** a picnic.
We They	**were**	

Note:
• Use the past continuous tense to talk about an action that was in progress at a specific time in the past.

C Complete the sentences about what was happening at the park yesterday afternoon. Use the past progressive tense.

1. The children (play) ___were playing___ on the seesaw.

2. A boy (fly) _____ a kite.

3. The children (ride) _____ the Ferris wheel.

4. A family (have) _____ a picnic.

5. Some people (watch) _____ a puppet show.

6. A cyclist (ride) _____ his bicycle.

7. A girl (buy) _____ a hot dog from the street vendor.

8. A little girl and her father (sit) _____ by the pond.

D **Write the correct answer from the box.**

Yes. It's a windy day.	~~Let's stop at the street vendor.~~
She's on the swings.	I made chicken sandwiches.
I'll go on it with you.	She fell off the monkey bars.
On the path.	In the trash can.

1. I'm hungry.   Let's stop at the street vendor.

2. Mom, can I fly my kite?   _____

3. Where should I put the garbage?   _____

4. Where is she jogging?   _____

5. How did she break her leg?   _____

6. I'm scared of the roller coaster. _____

7. Where is your daughter?   _____

8. What's in the picnic basket?   _____

CD 3
Track 25

E **Listen to each statement. Write the number of the statement under the correct picture.**

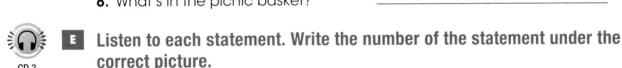

_____   _____   1   _____

_____   _____   _____   _____

Word Work **Partners**

Plan a local park. Include a pond, paths, a playground with equipment, and a picnic area. What other things will you include? Draw a map of your park. Label each item.

Places to Visit

A Write the names of four places that you can visit for free. Write four places that you have to pay admission.

These places are free:

hiking trail

_____

_____

_____

_____

You have to pay admission:

_____

_____

_____

_____

Grammar Connection: Present Tense – *If* Clauses

If you want to learn about the solar system,	visit a planetarium.
If you want to see that film,	it's playing at the local theater.

Note:
- When both clauses refer to the present time, use the present tense in both clauses.
- We can use *if* with the present tense to make suggestions.

B Complete the sentences with a suggestion of a place to visit.

1. If you have children and it's a hot day, _____cool off at a water park_____.

2. If you are looking for a bargain, _____.

3. If you are hungry, _____.

4. If you enjoy animals, _____.

5. If you are interested in history, _____.

6. If you would like some exercise, _____.

7. If you are a sports fan, _____.

8. If you want to buy flowers for your garden, _____.

9. If you want to learn more about the solar system, _____.

10. If you are interested in sea creatures, _____.

C Read each statement. Check *Possible* or *Not possible*.

	Possible	Not possible
1. You can see lions at an aquarium.	____	✓
2. You can ride the roller coaster at a nursery.	____	____
3. You can watch a sporting event at a stadium.	____	____
4. You can play pool at a museum.	____	____
5. You can touch the animals at a petting zoo.	____	____
6. You can lift weights at a rodeo.	____	____
7. You can watch the elephants at a circus.	____	____
8. You can use a computer at an Internet café.	____	____
9. You can swim in the pool at a water park.	____	____
10. You can buy plants at a video arcade.	____	____

CD 3
Track 26

D Listen to each speaker. Write the number of each statement next to the correct location.

____ **a.** amusement park   ____ **e.** circus

____ **b.** miniature golf course   ____ **f.** hiking trail

____ **c.** planetarium   ____ **g.** art museum

_1_ **d.** bowling alley   ____ **h.** aquarium

Word Work Small Group

Choose four places to visit. Write the name of a specific place in your area.

Kind of Place:	Specific Place in My Area:
museum	The Museum of Modern Art
_____	_____
_____	_____
_____	_____

Indoor Sports and Fitness

A **Complete the chart.**

Sport	Athlete	Place
basketball	<u>basketball player</u>	basketball court
_____	ping-pong player	ping-pong table
_____	boxer	_____
_____	gymnast	gym
diving	_____	_____

Grammar Connection: *How often ...?*

How often	do	you they	**go** to a sports club? **exercise**?
	does	he she	**play** darts? **wrestle**?

Note:
* *How often* asks frequency, for example, the number of times you do something every day or every week.
* Put *do* or *does* after *How often*.
* Use the base form of the verb in the question.

B **Write the question for each answer. Begin with *How often*.**

1. <u>How often does he use the treadmill?</u>

   He uses the treadmill every morning.

2. _____

   She swims three times a week.

3. _____

   They lift weights twice a week.

4. _____

   I take a fitness class on Fridays.

5. _____

   He plays ping-pong every day.

C Complete the sentences.

In our area there is a popular gym with many members. It's busy all day.

In the exercise room, people ride the ___stationary bikes___ or run on the

_____. Some people sit on the mats and do exercises, such as

_____ or _____. In the weight room, weightlifters

lie on _____ and lift weights. There is a large gym where the local

_____ team practices. In our area, _____

is the most popular sport and there is a room with twenty tables! In the

_____, people exercise to music. Lots of people relax in the

_____ classes. The _____ classes are always full

and many of the people have earned black belts. The newest addition is an

Olympic-size _____ with eight swimming lanes. After they exercise,

members can shower and change in the men's or women's _____.

CD 3
Track 27

D Listen to the information about each person's exercise routine. First, write the number of each speaker under the correct picture. Then, write the two indoor sports or fitness activities each person participates in.

_____

1

_____

_____

basketball

_____

_____

_____

_____

Word Work **Partners**

Imagine that you are going to join a gym. You will use the gym at least three days a week. List the days. Then, plan your exercise schedule. Describe your exercise schedule to a partner.

Outdoor Sports and Fitness

A **Complete the sentences with the name of a sports item from Exercise A.**

1. In football, a player wears a _____helmet_____ to protect his head.

2. In volleyball, players hit the ball over a _____.

3. Players can kick or head a _____.

4. In baseball, a player hits the ball with a _____.

5. In tennis, a player hits the ball with a _____.

6. In golf, a player hits the ball with a _____.

B **Write three individual sports and three team sports.**

Individual Sports	Team Sports
tennis	

┌─ Grammar Connection: **Adjectives with *one of the*** ─┐

I think	soccer	is	one of the most exciting	sports.
	golf		one of the most expensive	

Note:
• Use the superlative form of the verb after *one of the*.

C **Give your opinion about the outdoor sports in your dictionary.**

1. What do you think is one of the most difficult sports?

   I think _____

2. What do you think is one of the most tiring sports?

   _____

3. What do you think is one of the most exciting sports?

   _____

4. Who do you think is one of the most famous athletes in the world?

_____

5. What is one of the most popular sports in your country?

_____

D **Read each statement. Circle _T_ if the statement is true. Circle _F_ if the statement is false.**

1. In baseball, players hit the ball with a club.	T	(F)
2. A baseball player wears a uniform.	T	F
3. A baseball player catches the ball in a glove.	T	F
4. Soccer is played on a soccer field.	T	F
5. Many fans attend soccer games.	T	F
6. Soccer players wear helmets.	T	F
7. People play tennis on a golf course.	T	F
8. Tennis players hit the ball over a net.	T	F

E **Listen to each statement. Write the number of the statement next to the correct sport.**

CD 3
Track 28

_____ **a.** baseball

_____ **b.** track

_____ **c.** football

__1__ **d.** soccer

_____ **e.** golf

_____ **f.** volleyball

_____ **g.** tennis

Word Work **Small Group**

Discuss each sports team. How many players are on a team?

Soccer	_____	Rugby	_____
Baseball	_____	Football	_____
Volleyball	_____	Basketball	_____

Choose one sport. Write three rules of the game.

Winter Sports

A Complete the chart.

Sport	Athlete	Equipment
ice skating	ice skater	_____
_____	hockey player	_____
_____	skier	_____
_____	cross-country skier	skis
_____	_____	snowboard

B. Write the athlete who wears this equipment.

1. _an ice skater_   2. _____   3. _____   4. _____

Grammar Connection: **Statements with *used to . . . anymore***

I **used to** ice skate,	but I don't **anymore**.
He **used to** ice skate,	but he doesn't **anymore**.

Note:
- *Used to* talks about an activity or habit in the past that does not continue in the present.
- Use the base form of the verb after *used to*.
- Place *anymore* at the end of a sentence with *used to*.

C Use the words in parentheses to form sentences with *used to*.

1. (They / play hockey)   _They used to play hockey, but they don't anymore._

2. (I / snowshoe)   _____

3. (She / ski)   _____

4. (We / ice skate)   _____

5. (He / snowboard)   _____

6. (I / toboggan)   _____

D In your notebook, write about each picture. Where are the people? Write about their activities, equipment, and clothing.

1.

2.

3.

4.

CD 3
Track 29

E Listen to the information about each winter sport. Is the sport part of the Winter Olympic Games? Circle *Yes* or *No.*

1. ice skating   (Yes)   No

2. snowshoeing   Yes   No

3. downhill skiing   Yes   No

4. cross-country skiing   Yes   No

5. tobogganing   Yes   No

6. ice hockey   Yes   No

7. snowboarding   Yes   No

Word Work **Small Group**

Discuss or write the answers to the questions.

1. Which winter sports have you tried?

2. What equipment did you need? What did you wear?

3. Which sports look easy? Which sports look difficult?

4. Do you like to watch winter sports? Which sports do you like to watch?

5. When and where are the next Winter Olympics?

Games, Toys, and Hobbies

A Write the name of the game or activity under each item.

1. _____dice_____   2. _____   3. _____

4. _____   5. _____   6. _____

Grammar Connection: *I know how to / I don't know how to*

I **know how to** I **don't know how to**	play cards.

Note:
- *Know how to* and *don't know how to* talk about ability or skill.
- Use the base form of the verb after *know how to* and *don't know how to*.

B Complete the sentences about each game or activity. Use *I know how to* or *I don't know how to.*

1. _____ play chess.

2. _____ play dominoes.

3. _____ crochet.

4. _____ knit.

5. _____ embroider.

6. _____ build a model.

7. _____ play solitaire.

C Complete the sentences.

1. Chess and checkers are two ___board games___.

2. In checkers, the _____ are black and red.

3. There are 52 cards in a _____.

4. In order to knit, you need _____ and _____.

5. My son likes to build _____ of planes and ships.

6. Can you put together a _____ with 500 pieces?

7. Children like to color with _____.

8. Bridge is a popular _____ game.

D In your notebook, write about the pictures. What are the people doing? Describe the game or activity.

1.

2.

3.

4.

5.

6.

CD 3
Track 30

E Listen. Write the number of the card you hear under the correct picture.

a. b. c. d. e. f. g.

1

___ ___ ___ ___ ___ ___ ___

Word Work | Small Group

Bring a deck of cards to class. Teach the students in your group a card game from your country.

225

Camera, Stereo, and DVD

A **Complete the sentences. What kind of equipment do you use?**

1. ___You use a satellite dish___ to get good reception.

2. _____ to keep a camera steady.

3. _____ to take photographs.

4. _____ to play video games.

5. _____ to take pictures of people that are far away.

6. _____ to record a child's birthday party.

7. _____ to change channels.

Grammar Connection: Asking About Electronic Equipment

Does it come with	a case? a warranty?	Yes, it does. Yes, that's included.	No, it doesn't. No, that's extra.

Note:
• When you shop, ask about the features that you want.

B **Ask about these features on electronic equipment. Give a possible answer.**

1. camera / case?

   ___Does the camera come with a case?___   ___No, that's extra.___

2. camcorder / microphone?

   _____   _____

3. TV / remote?

   _____   _____

4. CD player / speakers?

   _____   _____

5. satellite dish / warranty?

   _____   _____

6. MP3 player / charger?

   _____   _____

C Match the statement and the response.

_c_ 1. I can't study when you're listening to a CD.

_____ 2. I'll take some pictures at the party..

_____ 3. That music is too loud.

_____ 4. I can't plug the TV in.

_____ 5. Do you have the remote control?

_____ 6. The music is too low. I can't hear it.

_____ 7. How can I listen to this cassette?

a. I'll turn it up.

b. You need an adapter.

c. I'll put my headphones on.

d. Yes. What channel do you want?

e. Use the stereo.

f. I'll turn it down.

g. Don't forget your camera.

CD 3
Track 31

D Each shopper is speaking with a salesperson in a store. Listen for the features that each speaker is asking about. Are they included? How long is the warranty?

Conversation 1: Camera

Battery Pack: Yes   No

Cable: Yes   No

Memory Card: Yes   No

Warranty: _____

Conversation 2: MP3 Player

Charger: Yes   No

Case: Yes   No

Headphones: Yes   No

Warranty: _____

Word Work Partners

You have the money to buy an electronics item for yourself. Which item would you choose? Who will show you how to use it? What electronics item would you like to buy for a member of your family? Explain why.

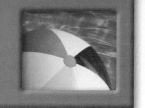

Holidays and Celebrations

A **Complete the sentences about each picture.**

1. Today is Jacob's tenth _____. He's going

to blow out the candles on his _____.

Then, he's going to open his _____.

2. Many families celebrate _____.

A few days before the holiday, families decorate a

_____ with _____.

On Christmas Eve, little children believe that

_____ visits their home and puts _____ under the tree.

Grammar Connection: Resolutions with *I will* and *I won't*

I will	walk thirty minutes a day.
I won't	buy any more shoes.

Note:
- Resolutions are promises we make to ourselves.
- People make resolutions on New Year's Day and try to keep them.
- Use the base form of the verb after *will* and *won't*.

B **Make a resolution about each of these parts of your life. Use *I will* or *I won't*.**

1. Health: _____

2. Money: _____

3: Family: _____

4. Work: _____

5. Leisure: _____

6. English: _____

CD 3
Track 32

C Listen to each conversation. Write the name of the holiday or occasion the speakers are talking about.

1. _____a birthday_____   4. _____

2. _____   5. _____

3. _____   6. _____

D Many people send greeting cards to their friends and families. Read the messages. Write the name of the holiday or special occasion.

1. A happy day to my special little monster. ____Halloween____

2. You're not getting older. You're getting better! _____

3. The office won't be the same without you. _____

4. I don't need a special holiday to say "I love you." _____

5. Congratulations on your new little one! _____

6. Today is a day for giving thanks for all the wonderful people and moments in

    our lives. _____

7. I have so many wonderful memories of growing up. You knew how to make me

    feel so special, so loved. _____

Word Work **Small Group**

Discuss or write about one holiday in your country.

1. What is the name of the holiday? When do you celebrate it?

2. What is the reason for the holiday?

3. What do you do on that day? Do you eat special foods?

4. Do you give each other gifts on that day?

Word Study

After you have a basic English vocabulary, you may want to buy a dictionary for English language learners. Choose a dictionary with clear, easy to understand definitions. There should also be sample sentences for each entry. Many dictionaries have pictures, drawings, maps, and appendices with notes on punctuation, grammar, and dictionary usage. Find a dictionary that will help you continue to build your vocabulary knowledge and skills.

Audioscript

Unit 1: Basic Words

Numbers
page 3

E. Listen and complete the forms.

Hello. I'm Jiang Xu.
My student ID number is 354-11-7832.
My cell phone number is 735-555-9480.

Hi. My name is Julia Hernandez.
My student ID number is 555-20-3961.
My telephone number is 908-555-3786.

Time
page 4

D. Listen and fill in the correct times.

1. The bank is open from 9:00 to 4:00.
2. The library is open from 9:30 in the morning to 10:00 at night.
3. The restaurant is only open for dinner. It opens at 5:15 and closes at midnight.
4. The supermarket is open from 7:15 to 10:30.
5. The post office opens at 8:30 and closes at 5:30.
6. The barbershop opens at 8:45 and closes at 5:45.

Calendar
page 7

F. Listen and write the month of each holiday from around the world.

1. Japan celebrates Tanabata on July 7th.
2. In India, people celebrate Diwali in October.
3. New Year's is usually in February in China.
4. Cinco de Mayo on May 5th is a popular holiday in Mexico.
5. December 13th is Santa Lucia, a national holiday in Sweden.
6. South Africa celebrates National Woman's Day on August 9th.
7. April 23rd is Children's Day in Turkey.

Money and Shopping
page 8

C. Write the price of each item.

A. A: How much is this pen?
   B: It's $1.00.
B. A: How much is this notebook?
   B: It's $2.50.
C. A: How much is this watch?
   B: It's on sale for $50.
D. A: How much are these flowers?
   B: They're $3.50.
E. A: How much is this stereo?
   B: The regular price is $125. But today it's only $100.
F. A: How much is the red umbrella?
   B: It's $5.00.
G. A: How much is this ball?
   B: The ball is $3.25.
H. A: How much is this hat?
   B: It's $10.50.

Colors
page 11

D. Listen to the description of each boy's clothing. Write each name under the correct boy.

I have six nephews.
Ben is wearing a yellow shirt and blue pants.
Jesse is wearing a white shirt, and he has blue pants.
Jason is wearing a red shirt and beige pants.
That's Todd with the violet shirt and the black pants.
Sam has a blue shirt and white pants.
And then there's Kyle. He has an orange shirt and brown pants.

In, On, Under
page 13

D. Listen to each statement about the desk. Circle *True* or *False*.

1. The pen is far from the book.
2. The pencil is on the desk.
3. The dictionary is on the left side of the desk.
4. The pencil is between the pencil sharpener and the eraser.
5. The pen is under the desk.
6. The eraser is in the desk.
7. The pencil sharpener is next to the pencil.
8. The dictionary is near the notebook.
9. The book is on top of the dictionary.

Opposites
page 15

D. Listen and circle the letter of the correct sentence.

1. My sister is three years old.
2. There's nothing in the box.
3. She can lift 100 pounds.
4. He's wearing a heavy coat, a hat, and gloves.
5. The baby is crying, and the TV is on.
6. I bought my car ten years ago.
7. Go and wash your hands!
8. He has two million dollars in the bank.

The Telephone
page 17

D. Listen to each sound or speaker. What is happening? Write the number of each sound or speaker next to the correct sentence.

1. [sound of a person dialing a number] - beeps
2. [sound of coins being put in a pay phone]
3. Good morning. Doctor Dean's office.
4. [sound of telephone beep on answering machine] Hi, Sam. This is Sue. Call me when you get this message.
5. A: I'd like to make a call to Japan.
6. [sound of phone ringing]
7. A: Directory assistance. What city, please?
   B: Atlanta. I'd like the number for Costa's Restaurant.

Unit 2: School

Classroom
page 19

E. Listen and write the number of each question before the correct answer.

1. Where's the chalk?
2. What's your teacher's name?
3. Where's the book?
4. What grade did you get on the test?
5. Where's Vietnam?
6. What's the homework assignment?
7. What time is it?

Listen, Read, Write
page 21

D. Listen and write the directions you hear.

1. Open your books to page 21.
2. Read page 21 silently.
3. Listen carefully and repeat the sentences.
4. Go to the board and write the sentences.
5. Discuss your ideas with your group.
6. Hand in your papers.
7. Close your books and take a break.

School
page 23

E. Listen to each statement. Where is each student?

1. I'd like a hamburger and french fries.
2. You can keep the books for two weeks.
3. I'm going to call your parents. You have a fever.
4. I need to change my schedule. I'd like to add an art class.
5. The score is 18 to 28. The Red Jays are ahead by ten points.
6. Listen to the conversation between the two speakers. Then, repeat each sentence.
7. It's nice to sit down for a few minutes. Did you give your students their midterm yet?
8. Students, for your homework, please read pages 20 to 24. Answer the questions on page 25.
9. Everyone, take your seats. I can't start the engine until all of you are sitting down.

Computers
page 25

E. Listen and complete the directions.

1. Press a key.
2. Send an e-mail.
3. Click on an icon.
4. Select the text.
5. Open a file.
6. Scan a picture.
7. Insert a CD-ROM.
8. Enter your password.
9. Surf the Web.
10. Attach the cable.

Unit 3: Family

Family
page 27

D. Listen and write the name of the correct person.

1. Who is Hiro's wife?
2. Who is Hiro's father?
3. Who is Hiro's son?
4. Who is Julia's sister?
5. Who is Eddie's grandmother?
6. Who is Yoshiko's aunt?
7. Who is Loretta's nephew?

Raising a Child
page 28

C. Listen and write the number of each statement next to the correct request.

1. He's hungry.
2. He's very tired.
3. He has a new book from the library.
4. He just hit his sister.
5. He can't walk down the stairs.
6. He has a wet diaper.
7. It's 8:00. It's time to go to school.

Life Events
page 31

D. Listen and write the number of each statement or question next to the correct event.

1. We would like to offer you the position.
2. That's wonderful! Have you decided on a date yet?
3. How long will you be in the hospital?
4. When we stop working, we are going to move to Florida.
5. We have tickets for a two-week cruise in the Caribbean.
6. She's beautiful! What are you going to name her?
7. How many rooms does it have?
8. Congratulations! You were accepted to the University of Maryland.

Unit 4: People

Face and Hair
page 33

D. Listen to each description. Write the letter of the correct man in Exercise C.

1. I have brown hair. It's very thick and curly. I have a beard and a moustache and long sideburns.
2. I have short black hair. It's straight. I wear glasses.
3. I have short brown hair. I have a moustache and a short beard. And I wear glasses.
4. I wear glasses. My hair is gray and wavy. I look in the mirror and I can't believe that I have wrinkles!
5. I'm bald. I shave my head two or three times a week. And I wear an earring in my right ear.

Daily Activities
page 35

D. Listen to Eric talk about his schedule. Put his day in order from 1 to 10.

Hi. My name is Eric and I'm a paramedic. I work the night shift, so my schedule is different from most people's. I get up at 3:00 in the afternoon and eat a small breakfast. Then, I go to the gym and work out for an hour. I take a shower at the gym. I go home and do my homework because I'm taking computer programming classes. Then, I make a big dinner and I eat at about 8:00 at night. After dinner, I watch TV for an hour or two. Then, I get dressed for work. I go to work at 10:15 and I work from 11:00 to 7:00 in the morning. I go to bed at 8:00 in the morning.

Walk, Jump, Run
page 37

E. Listen and complete the sentences.

1. I leave my apartment at 7:30.
2. I'm always late, so I run to the bus stop.
3. I get on the bus at 14th Street.
4. The bus is always crowded in the morning, so I have to stand.
5. I get off the bus at 53rd Street.
6. I cross the street and enter the building.
7. I go up the stairs to the third floor.
8. I go into my classroom. I sit down and take out my books.

Feelings
page 39

D. Listen to each situation. How does each person feel?

1. We have a big math test tomorrow. I studied, but chemistry is really difficult.
2. I just worked a double shift, from 7 in the morning until 11 at night.
3. Guess what! I got the job! The company called and offered me the job!
4. I'm sorry we moved here. I don't know anyone in this city. I don't have any friends here.
5. I'd like a tall glass of water.
6. I just can't get this printer to work. I've tried everything! But when I press Print, nothing happens.

Wave, Greet, Smile
page 41

D. Listen to each statement. Write the number of the correct statement next to each action.

1. Look at you! Nice suit!
2. I think so, too. He's the best soccer player on the team.
3. I'm having a party next Saturday. I hope you can come.
4. Adam, I'd like you to meet Sam. Sam is our new computer technician.
5. I'm sorry. I forgot to deliver the package.
6. Hi, Don. How's everything?
7. Hi, this is Jake. May I speak with Marcos?

Documents
page 43

D. Write the number of each question next to the correct answer.

1. What's your zip code?
2. What's your first name?
3. What's your e-mail address?
4. What's your city?
5. What's your date of birth?
6. What's your middle initial?
7. What's your last name?
8. What's your telephone number?
9. What's your state?
10. What's your student ID number?

Nationalities
page 45

D. Listen and complete each sentence with the nationality you hear.

1. Hot dogs are a favorite American food.
2. A French croissant is delicious.
3. You can enjoy delicious Italian pasta in many restaurants.
4. Russian caviar is the best in the world.
5. You can order paella at the Spanish restaurant in town.
6. Brazilian coffee is rich and flavorful.
7. Baklava is a sweet Greek dessert.
8. The new Japanese restaurant has wonderful sushi.
9. Some Indian curries are mild, but others are very hot.
10. That store sells delicious Colombian empanadas.

Unit 5: Community

Places Around Town
page 47

E. Listen to each statement and write the letter of the correct place.

1. How much is a gallon of gas?
2. Three tickets please, two adults and one child.
3. I have a reservation for tonight.
4. Your room is on the fourth floor. Here is your room key.
5. Could you put some air in the tires? And check the oil, please?
6. I didn't like the movie. It was too scary.
7. Please fill it up.
8. Mom, can we get some popcorn and soda?
9. I'd like a room for two nights. A nonsmoking room.

Shops and Stores
page 48

C. Listen to a woman talk about her trip to the mall. She went to eight different stores. Where did she go first, second, third, etc.? Put the correct number in front of each store.

I went to the mall this morning. First, I went to the beauty salon and got my hair cut. Then, I went to a clothing store and I bought a blue sweater. After that, I stopped at the toy store. It's my son's birthday, so I bought him a video game. Next, I went to the bookstore and I found a good mystery. I like to read mysteries. Then, I went to the pet store. I have ten tropical fish and I need fish food. I stopped at the jewelry store and I looked for a pair of earrings, but I didn't see anything that I liked. My last stop at the mall was the bakery where I bought a birthday cake for my son. Then, on my way home, I stopped at a flea market and I found a small lamp for the night table in my bedroom.

Bank
page 51

D. Listen to the information about World Bank and City Bank. Which offers better service?

There are two banks in my area, World Bank and City Bank. World Bank has ATMs everywhere. There is one across the street from my apartment building. City Bank doesn't have as many ATMs, but there is one near my work. I don't like the tellers at World Bank. They are not very helpful. The tellers at City Bank are friendly and helpful. I feel more comfortable there. World Bank gives 4% interest on savings. City Bank offers 5% interest. World Bank has drive-up windows and City Bank does, too. Both banks have safe-deposit boxes. At World Bank, a safe-deposit box is $100 a year. At City Bank, a safe-deposit box is $150 a year.

Post Office
page 53

D. Listen to the conversations. Write the word or phrase you hear.

1. A: Can I help you?
   B: Yes, I'd like a sheet of stamps.
2. A: Yes, how can I help you?
   B: I want to send this letter by overnight mail.
3. A: I'll be on vacation for two weeks.
   B: Send me a postcard.
4. A: Is there a mailbox near here?
   B: Yes. There's a mailbox on the corner of First and Broad.
5. A: What's the zip code for your town?
   B: It's 12817.
6. A: Where are you sending that package?
   B: I'm sending it to Spain.
7. A: When do you get your mail?
   B: The mail carrier comes at about 2:00.

Library
page 55

E. Where can each person look for the information he or she needs? Listen and write the number of each sentence under the correct picture.

1. I'd like some information about saving money for retirement.
2. What's the capital of Turkey?
3. I need some information about whales.
4. How do you pronounce this word?
5. I need a recipe for chocolate cake.
6. What's the weather forecast for tomorrow?

Daycare Center
page 57

D. Listen to this mother's schedule. Then, answer the questions.

My mornings are very busy. I'm a working mother with a one-year-old baby. His name is Ricky. He wakes up at 6:30. He's usually wet, so as soon as he wakes up, I change his diaper. Of course, he's hungry, so I give him a bottle. Then, I put him in his high chair and I feed him breakfast. After breakfast, I put Ricky in his playpen and he plays with his toys. While he plays, I pack his bag for the daycare center. He needs diapers, four bottles with formula, baby food, and, of course, his pacifier. I don't pack baby wipes, lotion, or powder because the daycare center has them.

City Square
page 59

E. A tourist just arrived in this city. Listen and number the places he went in the correct order.

I arrived in the city on Friday. I took a taxi from the airport to my hotel and I checked in. Then, I stopped at the tourist information booth. I wanted a map of the city and a bus schedule. They gave me lots of information! I sat down at a café, ordered a cup of coffee, and looked at the map and the information about the city. Next, I stopped at the bank and used my ATM card to get some extra cash. I also stopped at the travel agency to check on my car rental for the weekend. I spent the rest of the afternoon in the art museum.

Crime and Justice
page 61

E. Listen to the description of each crime. Circle the letter of the crime.

1. I just talked with our neighbor. Someone broke into his house last night and stole his TV and camera and computer.
2. Leo is really in trouble. First, the police stopped him for speeding. Then, he offered the police officer $100 to just "forget" about the ticket.
3. You know the Garcias? When they were on vacation, someone broke into their house. They broke a lot of the windows. They poured paint on their furniture. And they destroyed the lamps, the stereo, and the TV. Their house is a mess.
4. The police caught a man selling drugs on the corner near the high school.
5. You know the big fire in the school last week? The police found a gasoline can. They say that someone started the fire.
6. I hope the police put that woman in jail for ten years. She was drinking at a party, drinking a lot. On her way home, she hit a man who was walking his dog.

Unit 6: Housing

Types of Homes
page 63

D. Listen to each speaker. Write the number of each statement next to the correct type of home.

1. I live in a large town. My home is in a long row of houses. All the houses touch each other.
2. I live in the country. I get up at 5:00 in the morning to milk the cows and feed the animals.
3. I attend college. I live in a building with 300 other students.
4. I live in a small town. A truck moved our home to this location.
5. I live in a home on the water.
6. I'm 85 years old. I live in a building with many other seniors. Our building offers services such as a cafeteria and a small library.
7. I live in a large city. My home is on the 20th floor of my building.
8. I live in the suburbs. Our home has a living room, dining room, kitchen, and three bedrooms. We have a small yard.

Finding a Place to Live
page 65

E. Listen to Louis's story about renting an apartment. Put the sentences in order from 1 to 8.

Louis looked for an apartment for several weeks. Finally, he saw a nice apartment to rent. He signed the lease and paid the landlord a security deposit. The apartment will be available on Saturday.

Louis is going to get boxes from the supermarket. He's going to pack this week. On the weekend, his brother is going to help him move. They are going to load the van with boxes and furniture and drive to the new apartment. The landlord will be at the apartment building, and he will give Louis the key. Louis and his brother will carry everything into the apartment. First, they are going to arrange the furniture. Then, they are going to unpack the boxes. At night, Louis and his brother are going to order a pizza and relax.

Apartment Building

page 67

D. Listen to Sheri speak with her mother about three apartments for rent. Complete the chart as you listen.

Sheri: Mom, I looked at three apartments today. I don't know which one to rent.

Mother: Tell me about each one.

Sheri: Well, the first one is a studio. It's small, really small. But each apartment has a parking space. And the apartment building is close to work. I could walk to work. The rent is $700 a month.

Mother: What about the next apartment?

Sheri: It's a one-bedroom apartment, medium size. And the apartment has a parking space. But the apartment is on the first floor, in the back, next to the dumpster and the parking lot. The rent is $600. It's about three miles to work.

Mother: And the third apartment?

Sheri: Well, it's the nicest one, but it's also the most expensive. It's a one-bedroom, large and sunny, in a quiet area. But there isn't any parking. And the apartment is about 10 miles from work. The rent is $800. Mom, I don't know which apartment to choose.

Mother: What's the most important to you—the size, parking, distance to work, or the rent? You'll have to decide.

House and Garden

page 69

D. Look at the picture in the dictionary. Circle the correct answer.

1. Is the garage door open?
2. Is the lawnmower in the garage?
3. Is the sprinkler on?
4. Are the windows open?
5. Is the gate closed?
6. Are the shutters red?
7. Is the car in the driveway?

Kitchen and Dining Area

page 71

E. Look at the place setting. You will hear eight statements. Write the four statements that are true.

1. The plate is on the counter.
2. The plate is on a placemat.
3. The coffeemaker is on.
4. There is coffee in the mug.
5. The toaster is next to the coffeemaker.
6. The toast is on the plate.
7. There is bread in the toaster.
8. The mug is next to the coffeemaker.

Living Room

page 73

E. Look at the picture of the living room and listen to the statements. Circle T if the statement is true. Circle F if the statement is false.

1. The sofa is black.
2. The throw pillows are white and beige.
3. There's a coffee table in front of the sofa.
4. There are two armchairs in the living room.
5. There are curtains on the windows.
6. The blinds are open.
7. There's a fire in the fireplace.
8. There are two lamps in the room.
9. There's a rocking chair near the fireplace.
10. There's a clock on the mantel.

Bedroom and Bathroom

page 75

E. Listen to the speaker. Check if she is describing something that she likes or doesn't like about her bedroom and bathroom.

1. The closet is too small. I can't fit all my clothes in it.
2. We have a large, comfortable queen-size bed.
3. I use the large mirror on the back of the bedroom door every day when I'm getting dressed.
4. There's a new carpet on the bedroom floor.
5. The bathroom is very small.
6. The medicine cabinet has only two shelves. I don't have enough space to keep all my medical supplies and makeup.

Household Problems

page 77

E. Listen and look at the pictures of the bathroom and kitchen. If the sentence is true, circle T. If the sentence is false, circle F.

1. The ceiling in the kitchen is leaking.
2. There are mice on the floor.
3. There are ants on the counter.
4. The window is cracked.
5. The bathroom floor is flooded.
6. The toilet is clogged.
7. The ceiling is leaking.
8. One of the lightbulbs over the sink is burned out.

Household Chores

page 79

E. It's Saturday, and Lidia and Luis cleaned today. Look at each person's To Do List. Listen to the speaker and check the chores they completed.

Lidia: I've had a busy day! The house was a mess! This morning, I cleaned the bedroom and changed the sheets. I did the laundry. I washed the clothes and folded them and put everything away. Then, I cleaned the bathroom. I scrubbed the toilet, cleaned the sink, and mopped the floor. I wanted to clean the kitchen and cook, but I'm too tired. I think we'll go out for dinner tonight. I'll clean the kitchen tomorrow.

Luis: I had a lot of plans for today. This morning, I paid the bills. I emptied the wastebaskets in the house and took out the trash. I wanted to wash the car and mow the lawn, but I couldn't because it was raining. So, I watched a soccer game on TV. After the game, I vacuumed the carpets and polished the furniture.

Cleaning Supplies

page 81

E. Listen to each request. Circle the correct response.

1. Please vacuum the floor.
2. Please dust the furniture.
3. Please wash the dishes.
4. Please kill that fly.
5. Please wash the pots and pans.
6. Please clean the sink.
7. Please sweep the floor.

Unit 7: Food

Fruits and Nuts

page 83

E. Listen as the two workers put today's prices on the fruit at the farmers' market in Exercise D. Write the price of each fruit.

A: How much are the lemons today?
B: They're 50 cents each.
A: Okay, 50 cents. And the limes?
B: Same as yesterday. 40 cents each.
A: Okay. The strawberries?
B: We just got in a whole truck of strawberries. They're three dollars a quart.
A: Great price! And the apples?
B: Same as always. A dollar sixty-nine a pound.
A: Are the bananas still 59 cents a pound?
B: Uh-huh, 59 cents. But the peaches are on sale today. They're in season—a dollar seventy-nine a pound.
A: And the plums?
B: A dollar fifty-nine a pound.
A: Was that a dollar forty-nine?
B: A dollar fifty-nine.
A: How about the mangoes?
B: They're two dollars each.
A: That's about it. Oh, I forget the blueberries. Are they still a dollar seventy-five a pint?
B: Nope. Today they're down to a dollar fifty a pint.
A: Okay. That's it.

Vegetables

page 85

D. Listen to two friends plan a salad for dinner. Circle the items they will include in the salad.

A: I'm making a salad for dinner. I'm starting with lettuce and spinach and tomato.
B: I like mushrooms and pepper in my salad.
A: I have mushrooms, but I don't have any peppers.
B: Okay.
A: How about some onion?
B: Yes. But just a little. Do you have any celery?
A: No, I don't like celery, so I never buy it. Let's see, I have chickpeas, radishes, and carrots in the refrigerator.
B: The chickpeas are good, and I like carrots. But forget about the radishes.
A: OK.

Meat, Poultry, and Seafood

page 87

E. Complete the sentences with the meat, poultry, or seafood you hear.

1. We're having veal francése tonight.
2. The special tonight is scallops.
3. I'd like a ham sandwich.
4. A chicken sandwich, please.
5. We're having roast beef for dinner tonight.
6. I'll cook some steak on the grill.
7. I'm going to make meatballs with this ground beef.
8. The pork chops in that restaurant are delicious.
9. My brother is a fisherman. He often brings home fresh lobster.

Inside the Refrigerator

page 89

D. Listen to this couple write a list of items they need to buy at the supermarket. Check *Buy* or *Don't buy*.

1. There's only a little mayonnaise.
2. There's a lot of yogurt in the refrigerator.
3. We have only one egg.
4. There isn't much syrup in the bottle.
5. We have a lot of cheese.
6. There are three kinds of salad dressing in the refrigerator.
7. There is a container of milk, but it is almost empty.
8. We don't have any more jam.
9. We ate all the ice cream last night.

Food to Go

page 91

D. Listen to each question. Circle the letter of the correct response.

1. What kind of beans would you like?
2. What would you like on your hamburger?
3. What size pizza would you like?
4. What kind of rice would you like?
5. What would you like to drink?
6. Anything else to eat?
7. What do you put on your tacos?
8. What kind of potato would you like?

Cooking

page 93

E. Listen and complete the recipe.

To make chili you will need:
1 onion
1 tablespoon olive oil
1 pound ground beef
2 tablespoons chili powder
2 teaspoons cumin
1 1/2 cups crushed tomatoes
1 15 ounce can kidney beans

1. Chop the onion. Sauté in olive oil for 5 minutes.
2. Add the ground beef and sauté for 5 more minutes.
3. Add the chili powder and cumin.
4. Stir in the tomatoes and beans. Simmer for 20 minutes.

Cooking Equipment

page 95

E. Listen to each statement. Write the number of the correct item under each picture.

1. Put the soup in the saucepan.
2. Use a ladle to serve the soup.
3. Stir the soup with a wooden spoon.
4. Cut the onion on the cutting board.
5. Put the lid on the pot.
6. Drain the spaghetti in the colander.
7. Set the timer for 30 minutes.
8. When the thermometer shows 170°, the meat is done.

Measurements and Containers

page 97

E. Listen to each question. Circle the amount each person should buy.

1. How much orange juice do we need?
2. How much soap do we need?
3. How many potatoes should I buy?
4. How many apples do we need?
5. How much bread should I buy?
6. How much soda do you want?
7. How many eggs do we need?
8. How much yogurt do you want?

Supermarket

page 99

E. Listen to a customer ask about the location of each item. Circle the letter of the correct section.

1. I'm looking for the cat food.
2. Where is the toilet paper?
3. Where can I find dish soap?
4. Where can I get cold cuts?
5. I'm looking for yogurt.
6. Where is the chicken?
7. Where are the strawberries?
8. Where can I order a birthday cake?

Restaurant

page 101

C. Listen and write the name of the item that each customer is requesting.

1. I'd like a high chair for my daughter.
2. Do you have a salad bar?
3. I'd like to see the menu.
4. There is no pepper shaker on the table.
5. I dropped my fork. Can I have a clean one?
6. Can I have a glass of water, please.
7. I need a soup spoon.
8. Can I have another napkin?
9. What do you have for dessert?
10. Can we have the check, please?

Order, Eat, Pay

page 103

D. Listen to the story of Luis's first night as a waiter. Then, read each statement and circle *True* or *False*.

Mr. and Mrs. Park are eating dinner at Antonio's Restaurant. They made a reservation for 8:00. Luis, a new waiter at the restaurant, is waiting on them. Mr. and Mrs. Park ordered salad and a large pizza with onions and peppers. Luis poured their water, but he spilled water on the table. Then, Luis served the meal. He forgot Mr. and Mrs. Park's salad. He served them a large pizza with sausage. Mr. Park signaled the manager and spoke to him about the service. The manager is apologizing to Mr. and Mrs. Park. He is saying, "I'm sorry. This is Luis's first night as a waiter. Your meal tonight is free." The manager is going to speak to Luis. He is not ready to be a waiter yet. He needs more training.

■ Unit 8: Clothing

Clothes

page 105

E. Listen to each speaker. Number the two items each person bought.

1. I went to the mall yesterday. I bought a suit and a tie.
2. I found a very nice skirt and blouse for work.

3. It's my brother's birthday. I bought him shorts and a T-shirt.
4. I went shopping yesterday, and I got a jacket and a hat.
5. There was a sale at the store last week. I bought pants and a shirt.

Sleepwear, Underwear, and Swimwear

page 107

F. Listen and write the correct price under each item.

1. The slippers are $23.
2. The socks are $5 a pair.
3. The bikini is on sale. It's $35.
4. The camisole is $17.
5. The bathrobe is on sale this week. It's $45.
6. There's a special on baby items. The blanket sleeper is $9.
7. The nylons are $6 a pair.
8. The flip flops are $10.

Shoes and Accessories

page 109

E. Listen to the conversation between a mother and her daughter. Match the item and the location.

A: Ready for your interview?
B: I think so, but I'm really nervous.
A: You're not going to wear those sneakers, are you?
B: No, Mom. I have a pair of pumps in a bag in the car.
A: Good. Now, your hat and gloves are on the table.
B: I know.
A: And your purse is on the desk. Do you have your wallet?
B: Yes, I checked. It's in my purse.
A: Where's your briefcase?
B: It's already in the car.
A: You need sunglasses today.
B: I have them. They're in my coat pocket. Now, where are my keys?
A: I saw a key chain next to the TV.
B: That's where I left them!
A: Okay. You're all ready. Good luck!
B: Thanks, Mom.

Describing Clothes

page 111

D. Listen to this young woman decide which clothes to wear. Match the clothes that she is going to wear.

Conversation 1
A: What should I wear with my jeans?
B: How about your pink V-neck sweater?
A: It's warm today. I think I'll wear my pink polo shirt.

Conversation 2
A: What should I wear to the party? I'm definitely wearing my long black skirt.
B: I love that soft pink turtleneck you have. It's really pretty.
A: Yeah . . . I think that would look nice.

Conversation 3
A: What should I wear to work today? I want to wear my short beige skirt.
B: Wear your new pink cardigan. You look good in pink.
A: Thanks.

Conversation 4

A: I'm wearing my pleated black skirt to the movies.
B: Why don't you wear your pink V-neck sweater?
A: Good idea. I think I will.

Fabrics and Patterns   *page 113*

D. Listen to each conversation. Write the name of the pattern that the woman chooses under each picture.

Conversation 1

A: How do you like the paisley scarf?
B: It's nice, but not with a yellow sweater.
A: Which one should I wear?
B: How about the floral scarf?
A: Hmm. Yes. I like those together.

Conversation 2

A: Which scarf should I wear with this black sweater?
B: How about the solid yellow scarf?
A: No, that's too much solid. I want something with a pattern.
B: How about the striped one?
A: I wore that one yesterday. Do you like the paisley scarf?
B: I do! That looks great.

Conversation 3

A: I'm wearing a light blue sweater today.
B: I like the checked scarf with that.
A: I do, too. But I like the striped scarf, too.
B: Why don't you do something different?
A: Do you think the polka dot scarf matches?
B: Yeah, I think it looks nice.
A: Okay, I'll wear it.

Buying, Wearing, and Caring for Clothes   *page 115*

D. Listen to each statement. Write the number of the statement under the correct picture.

1. Take off your sweater. We need to wash it right away.
2. Amy, zip up your jacket before you go outside.
3. My button came off. I need to sew it on again.
4. Take off those dirty boots before you come in the house.
5. That shirt is wrinkled. You need to iron it before you wear it to work.
6. Mom, the zipper is stuck. I can't unzip it.
7. That shirt is too big for you. Roll up the sleeves.
8. Mom, where are the scissors? I need to cut off this price tag.

Sewing and Laundry   *page 117*

E. Listen and write the number of each statement under the correct shirt.

1. I bought a shirt today. A dress shirt with long sleeves. It has a collar, buttons, and a pocket in the front for a pen.
2. I bought a shirt today. Just a plain cotton shirt. No pocket, no collar. It's a short-sleeved shirt.
3. I bought a shirt today. I needed a short-sleeved dress shirt. It has a collar and buttons, of course, but it doesn't have a pocket in the front. I tried to find one with a pocket, but they didn't have any.
4. I bought a shirt today. It's a short-sleeved shirt with a collar and three buttons. And it has a pocket.
5. I bought a shirt today. It's a light blue shirt with long sleeves. It's very plain, it doesn't have a collar

or buttons, or a pocket. I liked it because it's soft and comfortable.
6. I bought a shirt today. Just a comfortable summer T-shirt. It doesn't have a collar or buttons. There's just a small pocket on the front.

■ Unit 9: Transportation

Vehicles and Traffic Signs   *page 119*

E. Listen to each statement. Write the number of the statement under the correct road sign.

1. You can't make a left turn here.
2. If people are crossing the street, you have to stop.
3. Drive carefully. We're near a school.
4. We are getting onto the highway. The other cars have the right-of-way.
5. We're coming to railroad tracks. Slow down a little. Look and listen carefully.
6. You have to stop.
7. You have to go to the right.
8. This road is narrow and has many turns. You can't pass any cars.
9. You can't make a U-turn here.
10. Follow the signs to the hospital.

Parts of a Car   *page 121*

D. Listen to a father teach his daughter how to drive. Circle the correct statement.

1. We're coming to a stop sign.
2. Turn left at the intersection.
3. The car isn't moving.
4. That car is going to pull out in front of you.
5. You need to change lanes.
6. It's starting to get dark.
7. It's starting to rain.

Road Trip   *page 123*

E. Listen to each statement and look at the picture. Circle *True* or *False*.

Picture 1

1. He ran out of gas.
2. He pulled over to the side of the road.
3. He had an accident.
4. He is getting gas at the gas station.

Picture 2

1. The driver is getting a speeding ticket.
2. The officer pulled this car over.
3. The driver has a flat tire.
4. The officer is washing the windshield.

Picture 3

1. He's lost.
2. He is looking at a map.
3. He pulled over to the side of the road.
4. He is asking for directions.

Airport

E. Listen to each sentence. Where is each person? Write the number of the statement next to the correct area in the airport.

1. Ms. Tanzer, you only declared one pair of shoes. I see ten pairs of new shoes in your baggage.
2. I need to see a photo ID and a credit card. Where are you flying today?
3. There it is. That black bag, the one with the big red name tag. Almost everyone has black bags, so I put that red tag on the handle.
4. Please remove all metal objects and change from your pockets. Take off your belts.
5. I need to see your passport. How long are you planning to stay in the country?
6. We are now seating passengers in rows 15 to 25. Please have your boarding pass out and ready to show the agent.

Taking a Flight
page 127

E. Look at the picture and listen to each statement. Write the seat number of the correct passenger.

1. This passenger is turning on the overhead light.
2. This passenger is stretching.
3. This passenger is stowing a carry-on bag.
4. This passenger is turning off her cell phone.
5. This passenger is listening to music.
6. This passenger is fastening her seat belt.
7. This passenger is putting on his headphones.
8. This passenger is finding his seat.

Public Transportation
page 129

E. Listen to each statement. Circle the type of transportation each person is talking about—train, subway, or taxi.

1. I took a taxi to work today because it was raining.
2. I took the subway to work today.
3. I gave my ticket to the conductor.
4. The fare on the meter was $7.00.
5. The fastest and cheapest way to get around the city is by subway.
6. I checked the schedule. There's a train at 8:30 and another one at 9:10.
7. I gave the driver a $2.00 tip.

Up, Over, Around
page 131

E. Listen to the directions. In your notebook, take notes or draw a map. Compare your directions with a friend. Listen again and check the directions.

A: Do you know how to get to Brook Park? I'd like to go this weekend.
B: Yes, I was there last month. Take 37 West. Stay on 37 West for about five miles. You'll go over a big bridge, the Grand Bridge. After the bridge, get off at Exit 6.
A: Okay, so I want Route 37 West and I'll look for Exit 6.
B: That's it. When you get off, you'll be on River Road, going south.
A: So, I want River Road.
B: Yeah. It's easy. You just go down the exit, and it goes right into River Road. You drive along the

river for about a mile. Then, you'll go into this little town, Chester.
A: So I'll be driving toward Chester.
B: Hmm, hmm. Go straight through the town; don't turn. As soon as you leave the town, you'll see the park on your right.
A: Thanks.

▇ Unit 10: Health

The Human Body
page 133

D. Listen to the directions for each of the three stretches. Complete the directions. Then, write the letter of each exercise under the correct picture.

A. Lie on your back with your knees bent. Slowly lift your hips and then your back off the floor. Hold for five seconds. Slowly lower your body to the floor, starting with your back.
B. Lie on your back with your knees bent. Keep one knee bent. Raise the other leg to the ceiling. Hold the leg with both hands and gently pull toward your body.
C. Lie on your back with your knees bent. Raise and bend one knee. Hold the leg with both hands. With your foot, make small circles in the air.

Illnesses, Injuries, Symptoms, and Disabilities
page 135

E. Listen to six people call in sick to work. Write the number of the conversation you hear next to the correct problem.

1. A: Ace Trucking.
   B: This is Bill Harding. I can't come to work today. I have the flu.
2. A: Board of Education.
   B: This is Ms. Gomez. I teach at Grove Elementary. I won't be in today. I have a bad stomachache.
3. A: Randy's Painting. Randy speaking.
   B: Hi, Randy. Mohammed here. I have a sprained wrist. It's my right hand, so I can't paint. I should be fine next week.
4. A: Mars Cars. How can I help you?
   B: This is Elena. My son has the chicken pox. I'm going to be out the rest of the week.
5. A: ABC Photo. Chris speaking.
   B: Hi. This is Lina. I don't feel well today. I'm dizzy and nauseous.
6. A: Harry's Rent-A-Car.
   B: Hi, Harry. This is Jacob. I have a bad cold. I'm going to stay home today.

Hurting and Healing
page 137

D. Listen to the conversation between a doctor and a patient. Read each statement and circle *T* for true or *F* for false.

A: I feel terrible.
B: Your blood pressure is a little low. And you have a fever of 102. Have you been vomiting?
A: No, but I've been coughing and sneezing. And I feel so tired.

B: You have the flu.

A: I thought so. Several people in my office have the flu.

B: You need to stay home for a few days. Get lots of sleep. Drink plenty of liquids, especially tea and juice. Here's a prescription. Take one pill in the morning and one at night. You'll feel better in a few days.

Hospital   *page 139*

D. Listen to the story about an emergency room patient. Circle *T* if the statement is true. Circle *F* if the statement is false.

Henry was driving to school yesterday when he was in a bad car accident. A witness called for an ambulance, and it was at the scene in a few minutes. Henry's arm was bleeding very badly. The paramedics stopped the bleeding and started an IV. They put him on a stretcher very carefully and put him in the ambulance. They took Henry to the emergency room. The doctor ordered an X-ray of his arm. It wasn't broken. A nurse cleaned Henry's arm and gave him a tetanus shot. Henry needed 30 stitches to close the cut.

Medical Center   *page 141*

D. Listen to each doctor. Write the number of each statement next to the correct specialist.

1. Tell me about your job. You are worried and angry about it.
2. Can you read the next line on the eye chart?
3. Congratulations! You're going to have a baby.
4. I'm going to put a small needle in your back. It isn't going to hurt.
5. You have a bad cough. I'm going to give you a prescription.
6. You need to wear the cast on your hand for six weeks.
7. You have a cavity in your tooth. It needs a filling.
8. The EKG shows an irregular heartbeat.

Pharmacy   *page 143*

E. Paul sprained his ankle. Listen to the story. Then, listen to the questions and write the number of each question next to the correct answer.

When Paul was playing soccer this morning, he sprained his ankle. Now he is at the doctor's office. The doctor is telling him to elevate his leg and to put an ice pack on his ankle four times a day for two days. After the swelling goes down, he should use a heating pad. The doctor showed Paul how to wrap his ankle in an elastic bandage. During the day, Paul should wear the elastic bandage on his ankle. When he walks, Paul needs to use a cane or crutches. If he has any pain, he should take aspirin.

1. What should Paul put on his ankle when he gets home?
2. What should Paul put on his ankle when the swelling goes down?
3. What should Paul wear on his ankle?
4. What should Paul use when he is walking?
5. What should Paul take for pain?

Soap, Comb, and Floss   *page 145*

E. Listen to Ava's morning routine. Circle the personal care items that she uses.

I have a routine that I follow every morning when I get up. First, I brush my teeth. Then, I take a long, hot shower. I wash my hair every morning, but I don't use conditioner because my hair is very short. It only takes me about five minutes to blow dry my hair. Next, I put lotion on my face because my skin is dry. I apply face powder and a little blush. I don't use any eye makeup in the morning. Then, I put on some deodorant and get dressed. After I get dressed, I brush my hair, put on some lipstick, and leave for work.

▇ Unit 11: Work

Jobs 1   *page 147*

E. Listen to each speaker. Write the name of the correct job.

1. I have the plans for the addition to your house.
2. I do quick sketches or take photos outside. I do the painting in my studio.
3. Your total is $27.00. Will that be cash or charge?
4. Would you like me to plant daffodils or sunflowers?
5. How large a chicken would you like? Four pounds? Five pounds?
6. What time should I put the children to bed?
7. We have a package for you. Please sign here.
8. How short would you like your hair?

Jobs 2   *page 149*

E. Listen to each statement. Who is each person speaking to?

1. I'm here to see Ms. Palmer.
2. There's a leak under the sink, and the water is dripping into the basement.
3. My car failed inspection. The left headlight is out and the windshield wipers don't work.
4. Ms. Ramirez, what is our homework for tomorrow?
5. I'm locked out of my house, and the keys are inside.
6. I'd like to sell all my shares of Royal Computers. And I'd like to buy 100 shares of Enerplus.
7. I'd like to go to the airport.
8. We're looking for a three-bedroom, two-bath home in Westwood. And we need a house with a two-car garage.
9. I can open and close my hand, and I'm making some progress with my fingers. I can pick up a pencil now.
10. We'd like to get away for a week, someplace quiet and warm, maybe Mexico or an island in the Caribbean.

Working

D. Listen to each person. What is the person doing?

1. I'm almost finished saving the information. I'll back up everything on a CD. Then, I'll check my e-mail.
2. [Woman singing]
3. Put your hands behind your back. You're under arrest for auto theft.
4. We've put ten sofas on the truck. Do you have any other orders for sofas?
5. This is our top-rated digital camera. It's easy to use. And, if you buy it today, you get 10% off.
6. Okay, Mr. Tremont. I have the information. I'll tell Ms. Georges as soon as she comes in the office.
7. Ms. Paulis, we'd like to offer you the job. Would you be able to start on the first of the month?

Farm

page 153

E. Look at each picture and listen to the statement. Circle *T* if the statement is true. Circle *F* if the statement is false.

1. The tractor is in the barn.
2. The farmer is plowing the field.
3. The farmer is watering the crops.
4. There is a scarecrow in the field.
5. The farmhand is working in the vineyard.
6. The farmer is picking the corn.
7. There are two farmhands in the barn.
8. The horse is eating hay.
9. One farmhand is milking a cow.
10. The other farmhand is feeding the pigs.
    The chickens are laying eggs. The tractor is in the barn.

Office

page 155

E. Listen to each request. Write the number of the request next to the correct item or equipment.

1. Please leave the boss a note.
2. Please sharpen these pencils.
3. Please file these reports.
4. Please put this memo on the bulletin board.
5. Please call the mail room.
6. Please correct this mistake.
7. Please add these figures.
8. Please write a letter to this customer.

Factory

page 157

D. Listen to each sentence and circle the letter(s) of the correct worker. If none of the workers is wearing the equipment, circle *None*.

1. This worker is wearing earplugs.
2. This worker is wearing safety boots.
3. This worker is wearing safety earmuffs.
4. This worker is wearing a hairnet.
5. This worker is wearing a safety visor.
6. This worker is wearing a safety vest.
7. This worker is wearing a particle mask.
8. This worker is wearing a hard hat.
9. This worker is wearing a respirator.
10. This worker is wearing safety goggles.

Hotel

page 159

D. Listen to the conversation between a desk clerk and a caller. Complete the information.

A: Hilltop Hotel.
B: I'd like to make a reservation for September 14th and 15th. We're attending a wedding at the hotel that weekend.
A: What size room would you like?
B: Well, it will be my husband and myself and our two sons. They're twelve and sixteen.
A: I could give you two double rooms, right next to one another. A double is $129 a night. Or, you could have a suite for $189 a night.
B: How big is the suite?
A: The bedroom has a king-size bed. The living room has a pullout sofa.
B: We'll take the suite. What time is the check-in?
A: You can check in any time after 2:00. And check-out is 12:00 noon.
B: Does the hotel have an exercise room?
A: Yes, we have a well-equipped fitness center.
B: And is there a pool?
A: We have a large outdoor pool.
B: Is there an extra charge for parking?
A: No. We have free parking. If you wish, valet service is available.

Tools and Supplies 1

page 161

D. Listen and write the price under the correct item in the hardware store advertisement.

1. A: How much is a blade for this power saw?
   B: A blade is $17.00.
2. A: How much is this hacksaw?
   B: The hacksaw is $24.00.
3. A: Are the extension cords on sale?
   B: Yes, they are. They're $14.00.
4. A: How much is the chisel?
   B: It's $11.00.
5. A: How much is this C-clamp?
   B: It's $4.00.
6. A: How much is the level?
   B: It's $9.00.

Tools and Supplies 2

page 163

D. Listen to this order for a hardware store. Complete the list of items.

A: Best Hardware. Sandy speaking.
B: Hi, Sandy. This is Bill Islip from Country Builders.
A: Hi, Bill. What are you working on today?
B: A bathroom. I've got a small order for you.
A: Go ahead. I've got the order form.
B: Okay. Six sheets of drywall and four sheets of plywood.
A: Uh-huh.
B: Two boxes of nails and three boxes of screws.
A: Okay. Two boxes of nails and three boxes of screws.
B: Hmm, hmm. Two rolls of insulation.
A: Okay.
B: Four door hinges.
A: That's four hinges?
B: Right. Just four.
A: And three packages of sandpaper. Medium grade.
B: Okay. Three packages of sandpaper.
A: I'll pick this up in about an hour?
B: Sure. No problem, Bill.

Drill, Sand, Paint   *page 164*

B. Listen to the conversation between two friends. Answer the questions.

A: How is the construction on your new home coming along?

B: Really good. I think it will be finished in about three months.

A: Did they pour the concrete?

B: Yes, the foundation is complete. And they dug a trench around the house for drainage.

A: Is the frame up?

B: Yes, the frame is up. And the windows have been installed.

A: Did they put up the drywall?

B: Not yet. First, they have to wire the house, and they haven't started that yet.

A: How about the plumbing?

B: They worked on the plumbing this week. I saw them cut and install the pipes.

A: Did they paint the outside of the house yet?

B: Oh, no. I'm not sure what color I want yet.

■ Unit 12: Earth and Space

Weather   *page 167*

D. Listen to the international weather report. Write the temperature and forecast for today and tomorrow for each country.

And now for our international weather report.

Call ahead if you are flying to Poland. It's cold today with temperatures below freezing. It will be quiet tonight, but heavy snow is forecast for tomorrow afternoon.

Australia is sunny and hot. Tomorrow will be cloudy. The hot temperatures will continue, but there is no rain in the forecast.

Japan is cool and rainy today. Light rain will continue into tomorrow. You can expect strong winds.

Beautiful weather conditions are forecast throughout Mexico for both today and tomorrow. Temperatures will be warm with no rain in sight.

It is raining today in Colombia. The rain will end by this evening. Tomorrow will be cloudy and hot.

France is experiencing colder-than-average temperatures for this time of year. Rain is forecast for tomorrow. Temperatures will fall below freezing, so expect some ice on the roads.

The Earth's Surface   *page 169*

E. Listen to the story of a long drive across the country. Write the nine features that are included in the story.

We went to visit my grandmother last summer. She lives very far from us, and we drove two days to get there. First, we crossed a low **mountain range.** Then, we drove across the **plains.** There were a lot of small farms. Next, we came to a wide **river** and took a long bridge over it. After that, we drove through a beautiful area with thousands of acres of **forest.** Then my family stopped for the night. The next morning, we stopped for extra water and gas to get ready for the road through the **desert.** We finally went over another **mountain range** and down to the **shore.** We waited for a ferry, and it took us across the **bay** to the small **island** where my grandmother lives.

Energy, Pollution, and Natural Disasters   *page 171*

D. Listen to the three conversations. Write the number of the conversation under the correct picture.

Conversation 1

A: Hi, Dad.

B: Patty! Where are you now? We just saw the news about the flood on TV.

A: We're at Aunt Naomi's house. We're going to stay here for a few days.

B: How's your house?

A: We're not sure. The police made us evacuate. The river is rising fast. But the rain finally stopped. Maybe the flood won't be too bad.

Conversation 2:

A: Hi, Dad. We wanted you to know we're fine.

B: I knew you would call us. How many feet of snow do you have?

A: We have three feet! It was hard to open the door!

B: Do you have power?

A: No, the blizzard knocked out all the power.

B: How long before you can get out?

A: The roads will be clear in another day or two.

Conversation 3:

A: Hi, Dad.

B: Kathy! We were so worried about you! We heard about the tornado on the radio.

A: It was terrible, Dad. I saw the black cloud in the sky. I took the kids, and we ran into the basement.

B: How's your house?

A: Our house is fine. But the people on the next block—it's terrible. Four or five houses are gone. The tornado just destroyed them.

The United States and Canada   *page 173*

D. Listen to the information about the national parks. Write the name of the state where you find each park.

1. Mesa Verde National Park is located in Colorado. Some of the first people who lived in this country built their homes in the cliffs.

2. Volcanic eruptions formed the Hawaiian Islands. At the Hawaii Volcanoes National Park you can hike to some of the world's largest and most active volcanoes.

3. You can take a boat trip through Everglades National Park in Florida to learn about the birds, animals, and plant life in this area.

4. Death Valley National Park in southern California is the hottest and driest place in the United States. Be sure to wear a large hat and bring plenty of water if you visit this desert area.

5. On a cruise of Glacier Bay National Park in Alaska, you can see giant glaciers. On your trip, you might also see whales playing in the cold waters.

6. One of the most popular national parks in the United States is Grand Canyon National Park in Arizona. Hiking to the bottom of the canyon and back up again is a two- to three-day trip.

The World
page 175

D. The world population is more than seven billion people. The pie chart shows the percentage of the world's population that lives on each continent. Listen and write the name of the correct continent on each part of the chart.

Asia is the largest continent, and it has the largest population. Over sixty percent of the world's population, more than four billion people, lives in Asia. Next is Africa. Nearly fifteen percent of the world's population lives in Africa. The population of this continent is growing faster than any other continent in the world. Next is Europe. Europe has eleven percent of the world's population. However, the population of Europe is growing more slowly than any other continent. Next is North America, including Central America. This part of the world has eight percent of the world's population. South America is next, with six percent of the population. Australia has the smallest percentage of the world's population, less than one percent. And what about Antarctica? Antarctica has no permanent human population.

The Universe
page 177

C. Listen to the information about the universe. Then, circle *T* if the statement is true or *F* if the statement is false.

The sun is a star, a bright ball of hot gas. It is the center of our solar system. The sun gives off heat and light. There are eight planets in our solar system, and all of them orbit around the sun in different paths. The planets don't travel around the sun in circles; their orbits are ovals. Mercury is the planet closest to the sun, and Neptune is the farthest from the sun.

Our planet, Earth, is the third planet from the sun. Earth's orbit around the sun takes 365 days, or one year, to complete. Earth also turns on its axis every 24 hours as it travels around the sun. As it turns, the area facing the sun has day. The area facing away from the sun has night.

Earth has one moon. The moon travels around Earth. It takes approximately 30 days for the moon to make one orbit around Earth.

▨ Unit 13: Animals, Plants, and Habitats

Garden
page 179

E. Listen to the description of each flower. Write the number of the flower under the correct picture.

1. This large flower has yellow petals. The center of the flower is brown, and it contains thousands of small seeds.
2. This easy-to-grow flower has a yellow center and white petals.
3. There are more than 100 varieties of this flower. It comes in many colors, but red and pink are the most popular. This flower grows on a small bush.
4. This flower grows from a bulb. It likes cool weather and flowers early in the spring. The flower looks like a small bowl. You can find this flower in almost every color.
5. This small flower is thick with hundreds of petals. It is usually orange or yellow.

Desert
page 181

D. Listen to each conversation between two people at a zoo. Then read each statement and circle *T* for true or *F* for false.

Conversation 1
A: Here's a tortoise. What's the difference between a tortoise and a turtle?
B: A tortoise lives on land. A turtle lives on land or in the water.
A: That's a really big tortoise.
B: Tortoises can get bigger than that. A tortoise can grow up to five feet long.
A: How long do they live?
B: A long time. Some of them live 100 years or longer.
A: I guess they don't have to worry about other animals attacking them or eating them.
B: No, they can just pull their head and legs inside their shells.
A: What does a tortoise eat?
B: Usually just plants. They don't have any teeth.

Conversation 2
A: That's a big owl. I didn't know owls got that big.
B: Yeah. Some owls are very large. It says here that there are more than 135 species of owls.
A: Owls sleep during the day, don't they?
B: Yeah. They usually stay in a tree in the daytime. Then, at night, they come out and hunt.
A: And what do they eat?
B: Insects, mostly, like moths and crickets. And small birds.
A: Owls have big eyes.
B: They do, but they can't move their eyes. That's why they turn their heads from side to side.
A: I don't see any ears.
B: Owls have ears, and they hear very well.

Rain Forest
page 183

E. Listen to each statement. Write the name of the correct bird or animal from Exercise D.

1. This colorful bird has a strong beak for eating fruit and nuts. It can imitate words and sounds.
2. This bird likes to stand in the water. It can easily stand on one leg.
3. This animal can fly, but it is not a bird. It sleeps all day and comes out at night looking for insects.
4. This is the smallest bird in the world. Its wings move very fast.
5. This colorful bird belongs to the parrot family. It is a favorite pet, especially the green and blue varieties. It has a long tail.
6. The male of this bird has a beautiful tail. It opens its tail and shows the colors to attract females.

Grasslands
page 185

D. Listen to the information about five endangered animals. Check the reasons why the number of these animals is decreasing.

Rhinoceroses are on the endangered species list. First, there is less and less land for these animals. Also, poachers kill the rhinoceroses for their horns. People in many countries believe that the horns have special powers. Each horn is worth $40,000.

The number of elephants is getting smaller each year. Elephants are losing their territory as more and more people need homes. Also, poachers kill the elephants for their ivory tusks.

Cheetahs are beautiful animals. Poachers hunt and kill cheetahs for their beautiful spotted fur.

There were once millions of kangaroos, but their numbers are decreasing. Kangaroos eat grass, the same grass that cattle eat. Ranchers and farmers kill kangaroos because there is not enough grass for all the animals.

Several kinds of zebras are on the endangered species list. Hunters kill zebras for their skin. Also, there is less and less land for these large animals as more people move into grassland areas.

Polar Lands
page 187

D. Listen to descriptions of these four animals. Write the number of the description under the correct animal.

1. This animal has large wings. Its tail feathers are black. It has a black head, a long black neck, and a white area on its neck and chin. Its beak is black.
2. This large animal has a thick body and strong legs. Its thick fur is usually gray or brown, and the fur around its neck and tail is white. It has a large set of antlers.
3. This large animal has thick white fur. It can swim, walk, or run. It has long claws for catching and eating seals and other animals. Its tail is very short.
4. This animal spends most of its life in the water. It comes onto land or onto the ice to sunbathe or to rest. It may be white, gray, or black. It has a rounded head, two large flippers, and a strong tail.

Sea
page 189

D. The ocean is very deep. Listen and draw a line from each ocean creature to the depth at which it usually swims.

Jellyfish like to swim or rest on the surface of the ocean.

Crabs also live near the surface. They will swim down to 100 feet below the surface.

At a depth of between 100 and 200 feet, you will see different kinds of sharks.

At 300 feet below the surface, you will find stingrays.

Sea horses usually swim at a depth of 400 feet.

At 500 feet, you can see tuna.

As you go deeper into the sea, the water becomes darker. At 600 feet, you can find octopuses. Also, a scuba diver can go down into the sea to a depth of 600 feet.

At 700 feet, it's more difficult to see. If you look carefully, you will see squid.

Woodlands
page 191

C. Listen to the description of each animal. Write the number of the description under the correct animal.

1. This small animal has long ears and a short tail. It has four legs. It uses its strong back legs to hop.
2. This bird lives on rivers or lakes. It has webbed feet, so it is a good swimmer. In the fall, this bird flies south where it is warmer.
3. This insect has a long, thin body and four large wings. Its body is often green or blue.
4. This large bird usually walks through the woods. Because it has a big body, it is difficult for this bird to fly. The male bird has a red or orange piece of skin on its throat.

5. This animal is a member of the cat family. It is usually beige and has small, dark spots. It has pointed ears and a short tail. It hunts small animals.

■ Unit 14: School Subjects

Math
page 193

F. Listen to each word problem. Write the numbers and solve the problem. What operation did you use?

Problem 1
Apples cost 99 cents a pound. How much do 5 pounds of apples cost?

Problem 2
A CD costs $12.99. Carmen has a coupon for $1.50 off. How much will she pay for the CD?

Problem 3
George has two part-time jobs. He earns $185 a week at the supermarket. On the weekends, he earns $160 as a housepainter. How much does he earn a week?

Problem 4
Five friends decided to go to a soccer game. Paul went to the stadium and bought 5 tickets for $75. How much did each ticket cost?

Problem 5
Cindy works 5 days a week. Her company is 11 miles from her home. How many miles does she commute each week?

Science
page 195

D. Listen to the science lab instructions. Write the number of the statement under the correct picture.

1. Put a drop of liquid on the slide.
2. Look at the liquid under the microscope.
3. Pick up the metal bar with the magnet.
4. Put the two items on the balance.
5. Pick up the items with the forceps.
6. Pour the liquid in the beaker.
7. Heat the solution with the Bunsen burner.
8. Use the funnel when you pour the liquid.

Writing
page 197

D. Listen and write the sentences you hear. Use the correct punctuation.

1. What time is it?
2. Stop it!
3. I don't know the answer.
4. He was born in Paris, France.
5. I bought everything for the party: the cake, candles, and balloons.
6. I can't work on Saturday, but I can work on Sunday.
7. The teacher said, "You're going to have a test tomorrow."

Explore, Rule, Invent *page 199*

D. Listen to the description of each event. Write the number of the description under the correct picture.

1. The Untied States launched the Hubble Telescope in 1990. It still sends back amazing pictures of the solar system.
2. China built the Three Gorges Dam, the largest dam in the world.
3. Alexander Graham Bell invented the telephone.
4. Airbus built a jet that can carry 800 passengers.
5. The Ericsson Company introduced the mobile telephone.
6. France built the Eiffel Tower in Paris in 1889.
7. The United Nations opened in 1945. The purpose of this organization is to establish peace and cooperation among nations.
8. Kodak invented the first digital camera in 1975.

U.S. Government and Citizenship *page 201*

D. Listen to each question and answer. Then, check *Citizen, Permanent Resident,* or both.

1. A: Does everyone have to obey the law?
   B: Yes, everyone has to obey the law.
2. A: Can everyone vote for president?
   B: No, only citizens can vote for president of the United States.
3. A: Does everyone have to pay taxes?
   B: Of course! Everyone has to pay taxes.
4. A: Can everyone serve on a jury?
   B: No, only citizens can serve on a jury.
5. A: Can everyone protest?
   B: Yes, everyone can protest.
6. A: Can everyone serve in the military?
   B: Both citizens and permanent residents can serve in the military.

▪ Unit 15: The Arts

Fine Arts *page 203*

E. Listen to the four conversations in a museum. Write the type of art that each visitor wants to see. Then, write the name of the correct section of the museum.

Conversation 1
A: I'd like to see the museum's collection of modern art.
B: You want section C, on the main floor.

Conversation 2
A: Yes?
B: I'm looking for the Mexican pottery exhibit.
A: You want section K, on the main floor.

Conversation 3
A: Excuse me. Where is the photography exhibit?
B: Photography is in section E, on the second floor.

Conversation 4
A: Can I help you?
B: I'm looking for sculptures—early Greek and Roman sculptures.
A: You want section D, on the third floor.

Performing Arts *page 205*

E. Listen to each speaker talk about a performance he or she attended. Write the number of the conversation next to the correct performance.

Conversation 1
A: I'm sorry I couldn't go on Saturday night. How was it?
B: The music was great! Wait 'til you hear what happened! About a minute after the music started, a cell phone rang. And . . . the conductor stopped the orchestra and turned around. He said, "Everyone, take out your cell phones and press off. When you're ready, we'll begin the symphony again."
A: Wow!

Conversation 2
A: How was the performance on Saturday night?
B: Wonderful! The dancers just flew across the stage. At one point, one of the dancers fell, but she got right up and continued dancing. Everyone in the audience applauded.

Conversation 3
A: How was the performance last night?
B: We loved it! Our seats were great. We were in the third row, right at center stage. We were able to see the faces, the makeup . . . the actors' expressions.

Conversation 4
A: I'm so sorry that I was sick on Saturday night.
B: Too bad you missed it. The music was great . . . the audience loved it! During one of the songs, the lead singer jumped off the stage and into the audience. He started singing to a girl who was sitting in front of me!

Instruments *page 206*

C. Listen and write the name of the instrument you hear.

1. [harmonica]
2. [cymbals]
3. [violin]
4. [French horn]
5. [flute]
6. [drums]
7. [organ]
8. [trumpet]
9. [guitar]
10. [harp]

Film, TV, and Music *page 209*

D. Listen to these lines from TV programs. On which type of TV program will you hear these lines?

1. We are going to bring you a live update on the continuing story of the train accident. Our reporter is on the scene. John, what are officials . . . saying about . . .
2. Should school systems remove all soda and snack machines from their buildings? We have three guests today who will discuss this issue, Doctor . . .
3. Kangaroos are one of the most interesting animals. They are found on only one continent, Australia. There are several types of kangaroos, from the . . .

4. Stacy, that was so nice! You shared your toy with Peter. Boys and girls, do you share *your* toys?
5. And now, we have one final question for our contestants. The first person to answer the question correctly will win the grand prize of . . .
6. Tune in tomorrow to find out if Emma will stay with Brian, or if she will leave him for Tony. And, will Adam learn that he has a brother . . .

Unit 16: Recreation

Beach   *page 211*

E. Listen. Check the items that this family is bringing to the beach.

A: Let's go. I have my surfboard.
B: You have your surfboard. That's it?
A: What else do we need?
B: Put the cooler in the car.
A: Okay. What do we need for Stacy?
B: Her water wings and pail and shovel are in the back of the car.
A: I'll get them. And her beach ball?
B: No, she likes to play in the sand.
A: What about the sunscreen?
B: I have it in my bag.
A: Should we bring the umbrella?
B: We don't have it anymore, remember? We left it at the beach last week.
A: We'll have to rent one.
B: Take two beach chairs and three towels.
A: What about your snorkel and fins and mask?
B: I'm not going to use them today.

Camping   *page 213*

E. Listen as a man and a woman pack their backpacks for a camping trip. Circle who will carry each piece of equipment, the man (*M*), the woman (*W*), or both.

Man: I have the camping stove in my backpack.
Woman: Good. Do you have the matches, too?
Man: Yes, I have them. And you have all the food, right?
Woman: I think so. I checked it carefully.
Man: Okay. I have the trail map and the pocket knife.
Woman: I have the compass and the fishing pole.
Man: Keep the compass in your pocket.
Woman: Okay.
Man: And we need our sleeping bags and air mattresses.
Woman: Right. And you have the tent, too?
Man: Yeah, I have it. How about your canteen?
Woman: I'm putting it on my belt.
Man: Me, too. Do you have the insect repellent?
Woman: Don't worry. I put it in an outside pocket. I would never forget the insect repellent.

City Park   *page 215*

E. Listen to each statement. Write the number of the statement under the correct picture.

1. This child is on the seesaw. His brother is sitting on the other side. They're going up and down.
2. This couple is enjoying a picnic in the park. They're sitting at a picnic table under the trees. They have

sandwiches and salad in their picnic basket.
3. It's cold outside, but these children don't care. They're going down the slide in the park.
4. This person is a good skateboarder. He takes his skateboard to the park every weekend and practices on the ramp.
5. These children are playing on the monkey bars.
6. The girl is on the playground. She is on the swing.
7. This man is a good skater. His wife just bought in-line skates, and he's teaching her how to skate.
8. These people are at an amusement park. They're riding the roller coaster.

Places to Visit   *page 217*

D. Listen to each speaker. Write the number of each statement next to the correct location.

1. Great! You got a strike!
2. This painting is by Van Gogh. He uses bright, active colors in his pictures.
3. Dad, what kind of fish is that? The gray one with the long tail?
4. It is beautiful up here on top of the mountain. You can see for miles in all directions.
5. Dad, I'm scared to go on the roller coaster. Will you go with me? Please?
6. This is Jupiter. Jupiter is the largest planet.
7. Ladies and gentlemen . . . And now in the center ring, I would like to introduce Zorba, the world-famous lion tamer!
8. We're at hole number 7. We have to hit the ball over that little bridge.

Indoor Sports and Fitness   *page 219*

D. Listen to the information about each person's exercise routine. First, write the number of each speaker under the correct picture. Then, write the two indoor sports or fitness activities each person participates in.

1. I play on the local basketball team. We have practice three days a week. Two days a week, I use the weightlifting room. I can bench press 150 pounds.
2. I have a stressful job and I go to the gym every day to relax. On Mondays, Wednesdays, and Fridays, I swim laps in the swimming pool before work. On Tuesdays and Thursdays, I take a yoga class after work.
3. I love ping-pong. I'm on the team at the gym and I practice two days a week. And I just started to take a martial arts class.

Outdoor Sports and Fitness   *page 221*

E. Listen to each statement. Write the number of the statement next to the correct sport.

1. The players kick the ball to each other.
2. A player hits the ball over the net with a racket.
3. A player uses a club to hit the ball into a small hole.
4. Players run down the field holding the ball.
5. The athletes run around a track.
6. The players hit the ball over the net with their hands.
7. A player hits the ball with a bat.

Winter Sports

page 223

E. Listen to the information about each winter sport. Is the sport part of the winter Olympic games? Circle *Yes* or *No*.

1. Ice skating is a popular Olympic event. There are three ice skating events: figure skating, ice dancing, and speed skating.
2. Snowshoeing is a popular winter activity, but it is not an Olympic sport.
3. Downhill skiing was one of the first Olympic sports. Thousands of people watch the skiers race down the hill.
4. Cross-country skiing is another Olympic sport. The skiers race over long distances.
5. Tobogganing is popular with families and children, but it is not part of the Olympics.
6. Most winter sports are individual sports. Ice hockey is one of the few team sports. Many countries send hockey teams to compete in the Olympic games.
7. Snowboarding is a new Olympic sport. The first snowboarding events were held in 1998.

Games, Toys, and Hobbies

page 225

E. Listen. Write the number of the card you hear under the correct picture.

1. the jack of spades
2. the ace of spades
3. the king of diamonds
4. the queen of hearts
5. the ace of diamonds
6. the jack of clubs
7. the king of hearts

Camera, Stereo, and DVD

page 227

D. Each shopper is speaking with a salesperson in a store. Listen for the features that each speaker is asking about. Are they included? How long is the warranty?

Conversation 1

A: This is our newest point and shoot camera. It's a 16 megapixel camera and it has a large three inch LCD screen. The pictures are amazing!
B: Does it come with a battery pack?
A: Yes, the battery pack is included.
B: How about a cable to connect the camera and the computer?
A: That's in the box, too.
B: Does the camera come with a memory card?
A: No, that's extra.
B: And the warranty. Does the camera come with a warranty?
A: Yes, there's a one-year warranty.

Conversation 2

A: We have a large selection of MP3 players, but this one is our most popular. It has a large touch screen and built-in Wi-Fi. You can access your music, photos, and videos. The sound quality is great.
B: Does it come with a charger?
A: Yes, that's included.

B: How about a case?
A: That's extra.
B: Does it come with headphones?
A: It comes with earbuds.
B: How about a warranty?
A: It has a 60-day warranty. But you can buy a full-year warranty for this model for only $15.00.

Holidays and Celebrations

page 229

C. Listen to each conversation. Write the name of the holiday or occasion the speakers are talking about.

1. A: Did you buy the candles?
   B: Yes. I bought two boxes. We need 21 candles this year.
2. A: Are you going to have your annual family barbecue?
   B: Yes, and then we're all going to watch the fireworks.
3. A: What costumes did you buy for the kids?
   B: Lisa is going to be a princess and Stevie is going to be a cowboy.
4. A: Did you visit your mother yesterday?
   B: No, she lives too far from here. But I sent her flowers, and I called her.
5. A: When are we going to buy the tree?
   B: Let's buy it on Saturday. We can decorate it on Sunday.
6. A: How was the party for Ella?
   B: Great! The company gave her a gold watch. Of course, it's going to be strange to see a different person sitting at her desk.